culinary
confessions
of the pta **divas**

Stylish Recipes and Saucy Secrets
for the Everyday Gourmet

Anne-Marie Hodges *with* Pam Brandon

To Alan, my meat-and-potatoes sweetheart,
and to Casey, my very best recipe for a son.
—Anne-Marie

For all the teachers who have inspired me.
For Katie, my little diva in training. And for
Steve and Will, the two men I love most.
—Pam

Copyright © 2005 by Anne-Marie Hodges
Published by Menasha Ridge Press
Distributed by The Globe Pequot Press
Manufactured in Canada
First Edition, Third Printing

Library of Congress Cataloging-in-Publication Data

Hodges, Anne-Marie.
Culinary confessions of the PTA Divas: stylish recipes and saucy secrets for the everyday gourmet /
Anne-Marie Hodges with Pam Brandon; photographs by Gary Bogdon.
p. cm.

ISBN 0-89732-624-5

1. Cookery. I. Brandon, Pam. II. Title.

TX714.H62 2004
641.5--dc22   2004059203

Text and cover design by Clare Minges
Photographs by Gary Bogdon

Table of Contents

acknowledgements

Special thanks to Aliette Scharr, the principal at Hillcrest Elementary, and Beth Conner, the assistant principal, who gave us carte blanche to be outrageous in our appreciation of their teachers and staff. To fellow PTA divas Susan Waldrip, Susan Gardner, Debbie Baker, Sara Isaac, Beth Gruber, Giselle Saindon, Marianne Vanness, Louise Craver, Kelly Magyar, Lisa Pardue, Georgia Fair, Elizabeth Eschbach, Sandy Butler and Erin Turner. To dads like Mark Gruber, Ed Butler, Ken Fair, Calvin Gardner and Roland Magyar who were always willing to pitch in and assist. To young teachers and friends like Alach Diaz, Kathy Mills, Kate Matson and D'Ann Rawlinson, and other teachers and staff, including Madame Perdomo, Ms. Le, Ms. Divine, Ms. Escobar, Ms. O'Leary, Ms. Cornelius, Ms. Hickey-Connell, Mr. Larson and Mr. Conner, who encouraged and supported our efforts. To Felicia Sherbert for teaching us about wine in her excellent guidebook. To Barbara Solomon at Oldies But Goodies Antiques in Orlando for her treasure trove of vintage wares. To Glenn Pace and Giselle Saindon for making us look like divas. To Tom Grzeszczak and Linda Hewett who graciously let us photograph their businesses. To the incredibly supportive staff at Menasha Ridge: Bob Sehlinger, Molly Merkle, Gabriela Oates, and Tricia Parks. To designer Clare Minges, editor Susan Roberts of *Cooking Light* magazine, and indexer Ann Cassar. And to our husbands, Steve Brandon and Alan Hicks, who give us their endless support and encouragement.

introduction

a nne-Marie deftly slices a perfect pork tenderloin. With a dollop of creamy polenta and a drizzle of balsamic glaze, it's a dish fit for an epicure in a four-star dining establishment. But instead, it's a dinner for 30 elementary schoolteachers, delighted with the unexpected VIP treatment.

Unexpected? When did a career in education start spiraling down to be seen as an undesirable aspiration?

We, the PTA Divas, were two businesswomen with a flair for the good life when we met in the Hillcrest Elementary school cafeteria in Orlando, Florida—not as schoolgirls but as moms. Our young sons were part of a pilot program at an inner-city school, a progressive attempt to teach foreign languages—Spanish, French, and Vietnamese—to students from kindergarten through fifth grade.

Our tale of food and friendship began with a grassroots crusade to uplift the status of dedicated teachers who spent nearly as much time with our children as we did. Hillcrest was a captivating melting pot, with a nearly even split of ethnicities: 25 percent black, 25 percent Hispanic, 25 percent white, and 25 percent Vietnamese. But with that diversity came poverty, students who lived in the projects, tiny children who came to school hungry and without shoes, and boys and girls who couldn't read.

Through the school's magnet language program, our children were among the first in Florida to be immersed in a foreign language at school on a daily basis. A short daily commute delivered our children to a fascinating global community worlds away from our neighborhood school.

At my first PTA meeting in 1996, there were six moms, $200 in the bank account, and high hopes. When my son commenced from Hillcrest, we had a rollicking PTA with more than two dozen active members and a budget of more than $10,000. Hard work? You bet. But the payoff—happy, appreciated teachers—is the greatest reward.

Since it truly is more blessed to give than to receive, we gave back with warmth and zeal. The PTA Divas were born when the music teacher, Ture Larson, asked for help hosting a winter holiday dinner for the teachers at his home. Instead of ordinary fare, we decided to make it fun, but also sophisticated.

We dug into our own pockets, rolled up our sleeves, and worked weeks in advance, preparing seared chicken in a rich tomato-cinnamon sauce, pungent feta and penne pasta, vegetables, and homemade pies. A cadre of moms arrived to serve and clean up—with several bottles of sipping wine for a thank you. The energy and camaraderie sealed lifelong friendships. A tradition was started.

With a fondness for food, we created and refined menus and succinct recipes. We made homey breakfasts, lunches, and dinners for underappreciated teachers. We got teary-eyed at their gratitude.

Teacher Appreciation Week became a much-anticipated event at Hillcrest, a week of lavishing teachers and staff, from janitors to the principal. And though we managed to acquire gifts for every single staffer, the one event they looked forward to most was the annual Teacher Appreciation Lunch, a lavish, crowd-pleasing extravaganza.

One year it was the Lizard Lounge, when we decorated the teachers' lounge to look like a 1960s nightclub, complete with a lounge singer in one corner. All of the PTA moms got in the spirit, dressing in tongue-in-chic garb. We served kitschy cocktail weenies and olive-cheese balls, and had the teachers jitterbugging on a makeshift dance floor.

Another year it was a Sunday Picnic on the school grounds, with fried chicken and all the fixin's, and all the moms in their mirthful Sunday best. Great times were shared as we built a community of parents and teachers with a foundation of love and laughter.

On morning walks after the kids were off to school, Anne-Marie and I would glamorize the life of our own mothers, with bouffant 'dos, a string of pearls, and smart dresses. We unabashedly embraced the values and styles of the 1960s, and our style was born—the PTA Divas, a common, multigenerational chord that made us grin, a sheer oxymoron in these days when most women consider PTA the domain of dull cookie bakers and wrapping-paper fund-raisers.

We decided to change the unappealing image, one good deed at a time. Our alter egos, Lulu and Verna Hicks, emerged as two wild-and-crazy retro divas who loved nothing more than cooking and dishing about the world around us.

We planned thank-yous, holidays, and milestone galas, and with each celebration came a new recipe, a new variation on a theme. Teachers asked for cooking classes, and some of our most fun afternoons were spent around the kitchen table with them, laughing, chopping, and sharing the joy of culinary discovery.

After five years at Hillcrest, Anne-Marie had a stack of her own recipes adapted to feed 50 or 60, and the idea for this cookbook was born—not necessarily for feeding crowds, but because she often was asked for a recipe.

Our confessions in each chapter offer shortcuts for from-scratch results, as we're probably cooking in a kitchen that looks a lot like yours. Ultimately, it's all about making life easier, and food fresher and healthier.

Although our sons benefited from Hillcrest, we too were enriched from the experience, with lifelong friendships and meaningful moments, with teachers who love us as much as we love them. We made it our mission to support and honor these amazing heroes.

Teachers deserve the best. Show them your gratitude. Remember when you were a kid—a teacher, no doubt, believed in you.

Cooking is joyous, and preparing food is an act of generosity. But what really nourishes us is our connection with those around us.

—Pam Brandon

PANTRY

It's time to move on; you've gotten way too comfortable in this relationship of convenience. Just a phone call, and there he is on your doorstep—your unwavering boy toy with the . . . PIZZA. A convenient pie of gooey cheese, pepperoni, and forbidden carbs. OK, it is delicious, but have you no pride?

Besides, cooking can be sexy, a libidinous feast for the senses that embraces everything from cultural diversity to time-travel memories of childhood. So step outside that pizza box and get creative. Put on some hip-swaying music and enjoy the art of nurturing. After all, it's only dinner.

You wouldn't wear the same pair of shoes every day, so think of your pantry as a trend-setting boutique of epicurean basics: fabulous beans, casual stocks, a designer vinegar or two. And let your collection stretch from the pantry to the fridge and freezer. Modify our lists to fit your family's tastes and then add a few baubles of your own: an exotic chutney, some off-the-shelf demi-glace, or a mack-daddy bottle of extra-virgin olive oil.

Imagination and a bit of planning are all it takes. Onions, celery, and carrots cooked in a bit of oil become a mirepoix, the aromatic French base for a gazillion savory soups and sauces. Toss in some frozen chicken tenderloins, a can of broth, a lavish pour of wine, and some herbes de Provence, and you've got a bistro-inspired stew. A dollop of mayonnaise, grainy mustard, breadcrumbs, and an egg transform superfood canned wild salmon into stylish croquettes. Or poach vitamin E–rich eggs in a simmering crock of your favorite spicy salsa for a lip-singeing plate of huevos rancheros. No need to drive to the store or super-size your thighs at the drive-through—depend on your capable cabinets.

We're not including everyday basics on our hit list, but those staples necessary for stress-free diva cuisine.

PRIDE

CHILLIN'

Butter

Carrots

Celery

Cheeses (such as feta, Parmesan, Cheddar)

Eggs

Fresh herbs (flat-leaf parsley, basil, cilantro)

Lemons

Lettuce greens or baby spinach

Mayonnaise

Sour cream

White wine, good enough to cook with

COLD AS ICE

Corn

Flash-frozen chicken tenderloins

Flash-frozen shrimp and fish

Frozen ravioli or tortellini

Peas

DRY AND CANNED GOODIES

Balsamic vinegar

Barbecue sauce

Black peppercorns and a good pepper mill

Canned beans (garbanzo, cannellini, kidney, black)

Canned green chiles

Canned hearts of palm

Canned tomatoes––chopped, crushed, diced, paste, and sauce––are a good start

Canned wild salmon

Canola oil

Chicken broth, beef broth, and vegetable broth

Coarse salt (kosher salt is terrific)

Dried herbs (herbes de Provence, basil, oregano, chervil, bay leaves, tarragon, sage, rosemary, dill, cumin, cinnamon, turmeric, coriander, cayenne pepper, white pepper, chipotle pepper)

Extra-virgin olive oil

Favorite hot sauces

Garlic

Green olives

Honey

Kalamata olives

Ketchup

Liquid smoke

Marinated artichoke hearts

Onions

Pasta (be creative and try penne, capellini, fusilli, pappardelle, bucatini, rigatoni)

Prepared marinara sauce

Red wine vinegar

Rice (we prefer whole-grain brown rice)

Salsa

Soy sauce

Sun-dried tomatoes, packed in oil

Toasted-sesame oil

Variety of mustards

Worcestershire sauce

BAUBLES

Capers

Chutney

Coconut milk

Couscous

Curry paste

Dried mushrooms

Nuts

Pesto

Roasted sesame seeds

Tahini

Truffle oil

Once you've stocked your kitchen, here are three fast-and-easy recipes you might try. Other pantry-proud recipes include Salmon Says Pantry Croquettes (page 99), Under the Tuscan Sun White Bean Soup (page 72), and African Queen Chicken with Tomatoes and Peanuts (page 113).

I'M CONFESSIN'

This is an easy recipe to double if you need to cook for a crowd. You may want to add a few tablespoons of your best quality olive oil just before serving, or some extra feta cheese.

SHOW-off SHRIMP and PENNE

"Oh, it was nothing … really." Imagine the cachet of tossing together this delicious one-dish meal at the last minute.

1 pound peeled and deveined frozen shrimp
4 tablespoons extra-virgin olive oil
4 garlic cloves, minced
1 (14-ounce) can crushed or diced tomatoes
½ cup dry white wine
2 teaspoons dried basil
Coarse salt and cracked black pepper, to taste
1 bay leaf
½ cup kalamata olives, pitted
½ pound penne pasta
½ to 1 cup crumbled feta cheese
4 tablespoons fresh chopped basil or flat-leaf parsley

Put salted water on to boil.

Thaw shrimp under running water for 2 to 3 minutes; drain and set aside.

In a large nonstick skillet, heat the oil, then sauté the garlic for one minute. Pour in the tomatoes and wine, seasoning with the dried basil, salt, pepper, and bay leaf.

Bring this sauce to a simmer and cook, uncovered, for about 10 minutes, stirring often. Add the olives and cook for 2 minutes; then add the shrimp and cook for about 4 to 5 minutes. Remove from heat. Remove bay leaf.

Cook the pasta until al dente according to package directions, reserving 1/4 cup of the pasta water before draining. Combine the pasta with the shrimp and sauce, adding a few teaspoons of the pasta water as necessary.

Toss mixture with the feta cheese and fresh herbs and serve immediately.

Serves 6

totally TORTELLINI SOUP

Picky children can relax: no floating bits of visible veggies to offend their inner purist. Just a home-infused broth with comforting pillows of cheese-filled pasta.

6 cups chicken broth or beef broth
2 garlic cloves, finely minced
1 teaspoon dried basil
1 teaspoon dried oregano
1 bay leaf
Coarse salt and cracked black pepper, to taste
¼ cup freshly grated Parmesan cheese
1 (8-ounce) package dried or frozen cheese tortellini
2 tablespoons extra-virgin olive oil
Juice of ½ lemon
Freshly grated Parmesan cheese (optional)

In a medium soup pot, bring the broth to a boil. Add the garlic, basil, oregano, and bay leaf; season with salt and pepper. Add the Parmesan cheese; simmer the broth for 10 minutes, allowing to reduce slightly. Taste for seasoning and add more salt if necessary.

Cook the tortellini in the broth until tender, about 5 minutes. Remove from heat; add olive oil and lemon juice. Remove bay leaf.

Serve with extra Parmesan cheese and a few turns of cracked black pepper if desired.

Serves 4

in a crunch SALAD

The queen of cool can toss together this crunchy little side salad in 5 minutes flat.

1 (14-ounce) can hearts of palm, cut into bite-size pieces
1 (14-ounce) can garbanzo beans
2 celery ribs, chopped
2 tablespoons chopped red onion
1 garlic clove, minced
2 tablespoons minced fresh parsley
Coarse salt and cracked black pepper, to taste
2 teaspoons red wine vinegar
Juice of ½ lemon
3 tablespoons extra-virgin olive oil

Combine all ingredients in a bowl; chill 30 minutes before serving.

Serves 6

haute and spicy

OK, we've all got them—those little containers of dried herbs and spices, some from this millennium, others definitely not. You buy them to use in one recipe, then ignore the remainder either out of fear—or dread. But whatever the case, we're here to shed some light on the subject, to allay your fears. Spice girls unite!

Herbs and spices impart an entire world of culinary "hip" without upping fat, calories, or sodium (or your dress size). Made up of leaves, seeds, roots, berries, and bodacious buds, they infuse cuisine with ethnicity and savoir faire. Dried spices need to cook or marinate before their flavors intensify, while fresh herbs lose their oomph after cooking.

Parting is sweet sorrow, but say good-bye to oregano that resembles sawdust. Store dried spices in airtight containers and discard them after a few months. To keep them fresher a little longer, toss them in the fridge or freezer. Wash and dry your fresh herbs before refrigeration and put them in a resealable bag in your vegetable crisper. Fresh parsley, cilantro, and basil should last about a week, thyme and rosemary a bit longer.

There are classic herb-and-spice combos that will remind you of your favorite dishes from around the globe. We'll give you herbs and spices that are easy to track down, but experiment with exotic varieties that you find in ethnic groceries or via the Internet.

> Herbs and spices impart an entire world of culinary "hip" without upping fat, calories, or sodium (or your dress size). Made up of leaves, seeds, roots, berries, and bodacious buds, they infuse cuisine with ethnicity and savoir faire.

SPICE ADVICE

FRENCH: Recall a cozy French bistro with a mélange of dried savory, rosemary, fennel seed, thyme, basil, tarragon, marjoram, and lavender—the classic herbes de Provence. You can find the mixture in gourmet grocery stores. Rub liberally on chicken before roasting, or toss with potatoes or veggies and roast until tender. Sprinkle into beef stew with Dijon mustard and wine. Fresh herbs that impart a similar taste include flat-leaf parsley, tarragon, rosemary, thyme, chervil, and marjoram.

ITALIAN: Most of us know the Italian basics—dried and fresh oregano, basil, bay leaves, thyme, rosemary, fennel, parsley, and sage. Start a fabulous red sauce with two or three tablespoons of dried basil, fresh garlic, canned crushed tomatoes, and extra-virgin olive oil. Support the flavor of the dried basil by adding fresh torn basil leaves just before serving (you can toss the fresh basil with the pasta or add it directly to the sauce). Rosemary, dried or fresh, is a natural wonder with garlic and fresh lemon juice. Massage into a pork loin, or toss with potatoes and roast.

GREEK: Here's our Grecian formula— oregano, dill, mint, bay leaves, cinnamon, rosemary, and parsley. Concoct an earthy, aromatic stew with chicken, pork, or lamb, crushed tomatoes, dried rosemary, and cinnamon, then garnish with fresh chopped mint leaves. Or fashion your next romaine salad with a handful of fresh minced dill and a sprightly lemon vinaigrette. Braise chicken pieces in long-simmering red sauce infused with cinnamon sticks, then top with crumbled feta.

MEXICAN: Olé! Pass the cumin seed, cinnamon, coriander, paprika, oregano, ground chiles, cilantro, and mint. Sauté chicken, onions, and peppers in a bit of oil with ground cumin seed, a pinch of cinnamon, oregano, and hot sauce for fajitas. Play with the amounts, and taste as you go. Throw together a homemade salsa with fresh tomatoes, garlic, onions, and jalapeño peppers—then kick it up with a pinch of ground cumin seed and several tablespoons of minced fresh cilantro. Fresh mint, though rarely used in Tex-Mex restaurants, grows wild throughout Mexico and is used liberally in soups, stews, salsas, and on roasted meats.

LATIN AMERICAN AND CARIBBEAN: A bit of a catch-all, but we include the flavors of the Caribbean islands and Central and South America. Splurge on saffron, the world's most expensive spice, used beautifully to flavor and color rice dishes like paella. In most grocery stores, you will find spice combos such as adobo––a blend of salt, granulated garlic, black pepper, and turmeric used to season chicken, beef, and rice. Shake it onto ground turkey, onions, garlic, a bit of tomato sauce, capers, raisins, and a splash of vinegar for tangy *picadillo*—heap over halved, roasted plantains for a lusty Latin presentation. *Sazon* is another friendly spice mix that imparts immediate Hispanic flavor. It can be found in some grocery stores, in specialty markets, or at www.goya. com. And though you've probably had your share, jerk, the pungent Jamaican spice rub featuring allspice and lots of peppery heat, is a must-try for backyard barbecues—serve the jerk of your choice with rice cooked in coconut milk for a sensory trip to the islands. A variety of ground chilies and interesting hot sauces are musts for Latin pantries.

INDIAN: The bomb, pure and simple. Nothing beats a plate of flavorful chicken curry—or shrimp in brilliant yellow yogurt sauce—and they're easier to create than you might think. Sauté curry spices with onions and garlic to intensify the smoky quality of Indian herb medleys. You can buy curry powder in any grocery store, but nothing beats fresh curry. To make your own, sauté a small minced onion in two tablespoons of vegetable oil. As the onion begins to caramelize, add equal parts fresh chopped garlic and fresh minced ginger. (Ginger paste, found in the produce section, is wonderfully convenient and lasts for several weeks in the fridge.) Being careful not to burn the garlic, add turmeric, cumin, coriander, and cinnamon, and sauté for one or two minutes. Toss in chopped chicken breasts, or beef, with a can of diced tomatoes. A pinch of cayenne will make the curry hot stuff. Simmer together until the meat is tender and the juice of the tomatoes is absorbed. Or try tilapia filets or Chilean sea bass in this easy, fresh curry. Sweeten the pot with garam masala, a traditional blend from Northern India, usually added toward the end of cooking or sprinkled on just before serving.

THAI: Favorite Thai herbs and spices include cilantro, sweet basil, mint, lemongrass, ginger, turmeric, and a variety of chilies. A simple, healthful Thai creation is turkey tenderloins simmered in coconut milk and chicken stock infused with lemongrass and a pinch of turmeric for color. Serve over rice with lots of fresh chopped herbs.

PINCH ME

Start cooking with a good coarse salt, and you'll never go back to the refined table variety. Place a small bowl of coarse salt near the stove and just use your fingers to sprinkle a small amount to season favorite creations. There really is a difference.

SEA SALT: With a bright, pure flavor and healthful minerals such as iron, magnesium, iodine, and zinc, sea salt is harvested from the ocean. It is believed to be healthier than table salt.

COARSE SALT: Coarse salt is a larger-grained sea-salt crystal. Both home cooks and professionals prefer coarse salt—it is easy to measure with one's fingers and easily stored for long periods. Use as a salt crust for meat or fish and to season stews, soups, and pasta.

FLEUR DE SEL: "Flower of salt" is the crème de la crème of condiment salt. True fleur de sel is harvested from the Guerande region of France.

KOSHER SALT: The diva of the margarita! Kosher salt is named for its use in

preparing meats to follow Jewish dietary guidelines. It has fewer additives and a saltier flavor than table salt.

SMOKED SEA SALT: It's new, exciting, and a must-try with grilled salmon. Salt grains are smoked over an open wood fire to infuse the salt crystals with natural smoked flavor. Use when grilling or roasting meats, or add an authentic smoky quality to soups, salads, sandwiches, or pasta.

BLACK SALT: This is an unrefined mineral salt with a pinkish gray color and a strong sulfuric flavor. Use it in Indian dishes.

WHAT ABOUT WINE?

We love a good bottle of wine. But it's easy to get confused perusing the aisles at your favorite wine store. You can always ask your wine purveyor for a good suggestion to accompany a dish. But in a pinch, here are a few simple rules to follow from our good friend Felicia Sherbert, author of *The Unofficial Guide to Selecting Wine*, and the quintessential wine diva.

SWEET FOODS: You might think that you eat sweet foods only during dessert, but the truth is that there is a fair amount of sweetness in many dishes, such as Italian tomato sauce, Japanese teriyaki, honey-mustard glazes, and the cocktail sauce you enjoy with shrimp. The sweetness in the food makes your wine seem drier that it really is, so you might want to go with an off-dry wine to balance out the flavor. Dry wine does not go well with sweet food. Try these good balancing acts for sweet foods:

White Zinfandel
Chenin Blanc
Riesling (an off-dry style)

FOODS HIGH IN ACID: These might include salads with a balsamic vinaigrette dressing, a main course such as fish served with a fresh squeeze of lemon (the acid ingredient), or a dish made with soy sauce. The acid in the food or the sauce needs a wine high in acid to balance the flavors. There are several ways to make a good match, depending on your personal preference. Try these good matches:

White Zinfandel
Sauvignon Blanc
Pinot Grigio
Dry Riesling
Muscadet
Pinot Noir

BITTER FOODS: If you love tricolor salads made with endive, radicchio, and arugula; if you can't get enough of the Greek kalamata olives; or if you prefer your meat charbroiled, you enjoy bitter tastes. The only challenge is that bitter food, in general, will accentuate a wine's bitterness. To counteract the bitterness in your food, look to these wines for balance:

Cabernet Sauvignon
Sauvignon Blanc
Pinot Noir

ASTRINGENT FOODS: Take a handful of nuts such as walnuts or pecans, throw them in your mouth, and chew. What does it feel like? As you chew the nuts, they act like a squeegee in your mouth and leave you with a dry, astringent feeling. The same is true for smoked salmon and those decadent chocolates you love so much. The best way to handle these foods is to meet them head-on with more tannic wines, which primarily are red, to break down these specially textured foods. To counteract the astringency in your food, try these wines for balance:

Merlot
Cabernet Sauvignon
Syrah
Côtes du Rhône wines
Nebbiolo

Wrapped, rolled, skewered, or stuffed, these enticing nibbles tease and flirt, but don't require a huge commitment. Finger food is for the fickle-hearted diva, so unplug the Crock-Pot®, toss the toothpicks, and boycott drunken weenies: make eyes at something new. Play the field with contrasting textures, flavors, and colors.

Start your party with one or two appetizers, or fill a table with a knockout buffet of light supper fare and be done with it. Pour the wine, pass the plates, and let guests' fingers do the walking.

ME UP

... BUNDLES of JOY

Mix it up and alternately wrap asparagus bundles with thinly sliced smoked provolone cheese. These are a colorful addition to standard antipasto platters.

Succulent asparagus wrapped in prosciutto snuggled under a comforting drizzle of rich balsamic vinegar and extra-virgin olive oil—these little bundles of yum are delicious.

1 pound fresh asparagus
¼ pound high-quality prosciutto, sliced very thin
Lettuce leaves
Balsamic vinegar
Extra-virgin olive oil
Coarse salt and cracked black pepper, to taste

Blanch the asparagus by plunging it into a pot of boiling water for 3 to 4 minutes. Rinse under cold running water to stop the cooking.

Divide spears into bundles, depending on the thickness of the asparagus —use 4 or 5 spears in a bunch if skinny, or just 2 or even 1, if very thick.

Wrap one slice of the prosciutto around each bundle and arrange on a lettuce-lined platter. Drizzle the bundles with balsamic vinegar and olive oil; season with salt and pepper. If preparing ahead, don't dress the bundles until serving.

Serves 6

MUSHROOM brie-CHETTA

A mushy romantic triangle between a chewy baguette; melted, gooey Brie; and a knockout mushroom ragout that defies all restraint. For a party, make the ragoût ahead of time, then just reheat.

2 tablespoons extra-virgin olive oil
12 ounces sliced cremini mushrooms
3 garlic cloves, minced
2 shallots, minced
½ teaspoon herbes de Provence
Coarse salt and cracked black pepper, to taste
½ cup dry white wine
2 teaspoons prepared demi-glace (available online or at specialty markets)
2 tablespoons fresh tarragon, minced
2 tablespoons unsalted butter
½ pound wedge of double-cream Brie (or triple-cream, but it's difficult to slice)
1 large baguette, halved lengthwise then cut into 4 pieces
Fresh tarragon (optional)

In a large skillet, heat the olive oil. Toss in the mushrooms, garlic, shallots, and herbes de Provence; season with salt and pepper. Stir in the wine and demi-glace. Add the fresh tarragon and continue to simmer for about 10 minutes until the mushrooms are tender and the sauce is thickened. Remove from heat and swirl in butter. Set aside on the stovetop, keeping warm.

Meanwhile, heat the broiler. Remove the rind from the Brie and cut Brie into pieces to evenly cover the 8 baguette slices. (If you place the cheese in the freezer for several minutes, it will be easier to slice.) Place baguette slices on a baking sheet. Broil for 5 minutes or until the cheese is bubbly and the edges of the bread are golden brown.

Place the baguettes on a platter and spoon the warm mushroom ragoût over the melted Brie. Garnish with fresh tarragon if desired.

Serves 8

• • •
I'M CONFESSIN'

Ragoût, or ragù? Don't let chichi kitchen terms confuse you. Ragoût is just a culinary term for a thick, rich stew. The word comes from the French *ragoûter*, meaning "to stimulate the appetite"— different from ragù, the meat sauce that's a staple in northern Italy, though both words are derived from the same French verb. The diva moves to the head of the class.

the beet goes on GOAT CHEESE AND PISTACHIO–STUFFED BOATS

Don't hold a grudge—it's time to embrace beets, your childhood nemesis. These ravishing oven-roasted beets aren't the homely variety Mom made you spend hours pushing about your plate. Like you, they're all grown up—ready to boogie down with toasty pistachios, bits of crumbled goat cheese, and slender leaves of endive.

FOR THE VINAIGRETTE:

3 tablespoons balsamic vinegar
½ teaspoon coarse salt
Cracked black pepper, to taste
1 teaspoon sugar
1 tablespoon Dijon mustard
5 tablespoons extra-virgin olive oil

FOR THE BEET MIXTURE:

4 medium beets
¼ cup shelled pistachios, toasted
4 ounces goat cheese, crumbled
Coarse salt and cracked black pepper, to taste
1 head Belgian endive, leaves separated and rinsed

Preheat oven to 400°.

To prepare the vinaigrette, in a small bowl, combine the vinegar, salt, pepper, and sugar, stirring with a whisk. Whisk in the mustard. Slowly add olive oil, whisking until well mixed. Set aside.

To prepare the beet mixture, scrub the unpeeled beets and bake at 400° until easily pierced with a knife. A large beet may need to bake up to an hour, smaller beets, 25 to 30 minutes. Cool, skin, and dice. (Beets can be roasted ahead of time).

Combine the beets, pistachios, and goat cheese. Mix in the vinaigrette and season with salt and pepper. Spoon the beet mixture into the Belgian endive leaves.

Serves 8

sea and be seen SEA BASS CEVICHE

This South American star drips with style. Bejeweled with red chiles and flavorful herbs, pearl-white slivers of Chilean sea bass bathe in a summery fusion of lemon and lime juices. Beat the heat and entertain with ease as the lime juice "cooks" this healthful dish in the fridge.

2 pounds Chilean sea bass, all bones removed
Juice of 2 large lemons, or 3 small
Juice of 4 to 6 limes
½ red onion, thinly sliced and separated into rings
1 garlic clove, minced
1 hot red chile, seeded and cut into thin strips
1 sweet orange pepper, cut into thin strips
2 tablespoons fresh flat-leaf parsley, chopped
3 tablespoons fresh cilantro, minced
Salt and pepper, to taste
Extra-virgin olive oil, to taste
6 ripe Hass avocados, halved, peeled, and pitted

Rinse the fish; pat dry and slice thinly into bite-size pieces.

In a 2-quart stainless steel bowl, combine the citrus juices, onion, garlic, chile, orange pepper, and fresh herbs.

Add the sea bass, making sure the citrus mixture generously covers the fish. Season with salt and pepper.

Allow the fish to marinate, or "cook," in the fridge for at least 4 hours—until the fish no longer looks raw. Season if desired and drizzle with a bit of olive oil. Serve in avocado halves.

Serves 8

• • •

I'M CONFESSIN'

For instant gratifica-
tion, experiment with
store-bought sauces.
Fabulous chipotle
concoctions are all the
rage on the shelves at
most grocery stores.

bold and beautiful BACON-WRAPPED SCALLOP and SALMON SKEWERS

We've followed this drama for years: pleasingly plump sea scallops wrapped in crisp, sizzling bacon. Seen at all the parties, who could resist this dynamic duo that proves opposites really do attract? But here's the twist. Their tried-and-true relationship gets a shake-up with sexy chunks of color-rich salmon—and the brazen bacon sizzles with both.

½ pound sea scallops
1 pound salmon fillets
6 skewers
½ pound bacon
Maple Chipotle Glaze (see recipe below)
Juice of 1 large lime

Preheat oven to 450°.

Rinse scallops and discard any white membrane (that held the flesh to the shell). Cut salmon into chunks roughly the same size as the scallops.

If using wooden skewers, soak them in water for 10 to 15 minutes while you prepare the glaze.

Cut bacon slices in half, about 4 inches long. Wrap the scallops and salmon bites with the bacon, threading them alternately onto the skewers. Brush the skewers liberally with maple/chipotle glaze.

In a shallow baking dish, bake at 450° for 20 minutes or until the bacon is crisp. (Lining the baking dish with foil makes clean-up a breeze.)

Drizzle with lime juice and serve immediately.

MAPLE CHIPOTLE GLAZE
½ cup maple syrup
2 tablespoons Dijon mustard
2 tablespoons adobo sauce (from small can chipotle chiles)

Serves 6

PUCKER up LEMONY CRAB RELISH

Relish this summer romance of crab, red chiles, baby arugula, and a kiss of fresh lemon. Mound onto avocado halves or crusty cuts of French bread. Serve this as a starter or as a light meal. Or pair with gazpacho and Never Too Thin Chilled Sliced Beef with Tomato-Basil Salsa (page 28) for a lovely summer buffet.

3 garlic cloves
1 teaspoon kosher salt
2 fresh red chiles, seeded and chopped
1 pound crabmeat, shell pieces removed
¼ cup extra-virgin olive oil
Juice of 1 lemon
Lemon zest, to taste
1 cup baby arugula leaves, coarsely chopped
3 tablespoons minced fresh parsley
Fresh avocados, halved, or fresh French bread, torn into chunks

Using a mortar and pestle, pound the garlic along with the salt until a smooth paste is formed; transfer to a large mixing bowl.

Add the red chiles, crab, olive oil, lemon juice, and lemon zest; gently mix. Add the arugula and parsley just before serving.

Serve in avocado halves, or mound on a platter and serve with bread.

Serves 10

● ● ●

I'M CONFESSIN'

Those little red chiles add a nice bite to this salad. If you prefer the taste and not the heat, remove the seeds and veins—and wash your hands after chopping. The fiery capsaicin in the chile can burn your eyes or skin.

TALK of the TOWN TURKEY PÂTÉ

Serve this pâté rustica with fashionably crusty bread, good olives, cornichon pickles, and grainy mustard—it's also rumored to make a sensational sandwich. And if you're wondering, a cornichon is just a teensy French pickle with huge flavor. They're superbly sour, and you can sometimes find the fresh variety at gourmet markets—or check out the gourmet jarred pickles.

Class with sass is affordable when ground turkey, turkey sausage, pistachios, and tarragon come together in an unusual country pâté that will have them all talking. (And it's healthier than the stuff your mom used to serve.)

1 pound ground turkey (dark and white meat)
½ pound turkey sausage
1 egg
1 cup sourdough breadcrumbs
½ cup shelled pistachios
2 tablespoons Dijon mustard
1 teaspoon Worcestershire sauce
2 teaspoons dried fine herbs, such as chervil, marjoram, chives, and basil
3 tablespoons fresh tarragon, chopped
2 garlic cloves, minced
Salt and freshly ground black pepper, to taste
8 fresh bay leaves

Preheat oven to 325°.

Combine all the ingredients in a large bowl; mix with your hands.

Press the mixture into a 9 x 5–inch loaf pan, filling the corners completely. Turn the loaf out onto a large casserole or baking sheet. Press the bay leaves into the top of the loaf in a decorative manner, and grind a bit more pepper over the top.

Bake, uncovered, at 325° for 1½ hours. Let stand at least 10 minutes before serving. Delicious served cold.

Serves 12

LIVE and let LIVER PÂTÉ

It's no secret—chicken livers are the misunderstood beauties of the poultry case. Dark and dangerous, their suitors boast a certain bravery, a willingness to stray from the pack—to embrace the old adage that beauty is, indeed, in the eye of the beholder.

1 pound chicken livers, rinsed, tough parts removed
1 onion, thinly sliced
2 cups chicken stock
1 bay leaf
Salt and pepper, to taste
3 slices turkey bacon
½ to 1 cup shelled pistachios
1 teaspoon Dijon mustard
3 tablespoons sherry
2 teaspoons dried tarragon
2 tablespoons fresh flat-leaf parsley, minced
½ stick unsalted butter, softened
1 teaspoon fresh lemon juice

Combine the livers, onion, chicken stock, and bay leaf in a medium saucepan. Season with salt and pepper. Simmer until the livers are tender and no longer pink in the center.

Cook the bacon until crisp; drain on paper towels and crumble.

Discard the onion and the bay leaf and drain the livers. In a food processor or blender, combine the livers, bacon, pistachios, mustard, sherry, tarragon, parsley, butter, and lemon juice. Pulse until smooth. Taste and adjust the seasoning if necessary. Add additional herbs and sherry if desired.

Lightly grease your hands and form the liver mixture into a mound. Chill for at least 2 hours.

Serves 10 to 12

● ● ●

I'M CONFESSIN'

We've pumped up the spices and used less fat than a classic pâté. Most liver pâtés call for two sticks of butter—we're using just one half stick. Serve with bread or crackers, grainy mustard, and cornichons.

never too thin CHILLED SLICED BEEF with TOMATO-BASIL SALSA

Skinny slices of chilled steak are coiffured in fresh tomato-and-basil salsa for a low-carb sweetheart for a summer picnic—a do-ahead diva's closest chum.

1 (2-pound) top sirloin steak
Kosher salt and freshly ground black pepper, to taste
1 tablespoon herbes de Provence
6 tablespoons extra-virgin olive oil, divided
1 pint grape tomatoes, halved
12 large basil leaves, thinly sliced
4 garlic cloves, minced
1 teaspoon fresh lemon juice

Season the steak with kosher salt and freshly ground black pepper. Rub with herbes de Provence.

Heat a large skillet over medium-to-high heat and add 3 tablespoons of olive oil. When the oil is hot, sear the meat about 5 minutes on each side. (Although this dish is best with rare meat, you may cook the steak longer if you prefer.) Transfer the meat to a platter and cool. Refrigerate until you're ready to serve.

Combine the tomatoes, basil, garlic, lemon juice, and remaining 3 tablespoons of olive oil, and toss.

With a sharp knife, thinly slice the meat on a diagonal and arrange on a serving platter. Top with the salsa. Season again with salt and pepper to taste.

Serves 8

pinnacle of PROSCIUTTO SANDWICHES

Forget bologna. Toast a chewy baguette and fill it with these contrasting flavors and textures for a melt-in-your-mouth creation that's huge on style—not on time. This makes a meal—or slice and serve for party food.

6 plum tomatoes
¼ cup extra-virgin olive oil, divided
Salt and pepper, to taste
2 baguettes (15 to 17 inches long)
8 slices fresh mozzarella (¼ inch thick)
12 slices prosciutto
2 cups arugula
2 teaspoons red wine vinegar

Preheat oven to 300°.

Cut the tomatoes in half, brush with olive oil, and season with salt and pepper. Bake at 300° for about 2 hours until the tomatoes shrivel, the edges start to turn brown, and most of the liquid around the tomatoes has caramelized. Set aside.

Slice the baguettes in half lengthwise and lightly brush both sides with olive oil. Layer the bottom halves with the tomatoes, cheese, prosciutto, and arugula. Drizzle with a bit more oil, then sprinkle with red wine vinegar, salt, and pepper to taste. Top with the top halves, wrap in foil, and heat for a few minutes before serving if desired.

Serves 12

● ● ●

I'M CONFESSIN'

Shop for fresh mozzarella, generally made from whole milk, and softer and sweeter than regular mozzarella.

I'M CONFESSIN'

You could substitute provolone for the fresh mozzarella. And if you don't care for pepperoni, try any other favorite Italian cold cuts, like Genoa salami.

call me sophia FRESH MOZZARELLA and PEPPERONI BRUSCHETTA

Draped in fashionable tomato vinaigrette and surrounded by chunks of crusty Italian bread, this full-figured mound of fresh mozzarella, pepperoni, veggies, and torn basil is, well, lust in a bowl. Grab a fork and give in to desire.

Call Me Sophia Italian Tomato Vinaigrette (page 137)
8 ounces fresh mozzarella
8 ounces pepperoni, casings removed
1 cup sliced cremini mushrooms
1 red bell pepper, chopped
½ red onion, finely chopped
4 plum tomatoes, seeded and chopped
12 fresh basil leaves, torn into small pieces
1 large baguette
Extra-virgin olive oil

Dice the mozzarella and pepperoni into ½-inch chunks. In a large bowl, combine with mushrooms, bell pepper, onion, tomatoes, and basil. Drizzle with vinaigrette. Heap onto a platter and surround with sliced or torn bread.

Drizzle with a little extra-virgin olive oil. If preparing ahead, add the basil just before serving so it won't wilt and darken.

Serves 10

WRAP-turous WRAPS

Fickle-hearted divas, this is your finger food—delicious bits of this and that rolled in thin, pliable tortillas or flatbreads, then sliced just big enough for a bite or two. And no two creations are ever the same with wraps in several different flavors and colors, from pesto and lemon to spinach and tomato.

ROAST CHICKEN AND CHUTNEY WRAPS

1 package of 6 large wraps or flour tortillas, flavored or plain
1 (8-ounce) container spreadable cheese with herbs
2 roasted chicken breasts, deboned, sliced, and divided into 6 portions
6 tablespoons prepared corn-and-pepper chutney, or corn relish
       (available in most grocery store condiment sections)
1½ cups chopped romaine lettuce
½ cup finely diced red onion
½ cup chopped fresh cilantro
½ cup fried crumbled bacon

Spread 1 tortilla with about 2 tablespoons cheese with herbs, making sure the top edge is covered—this will be the "glue" that holds the wrap together.

Starting on the side closet to you, place one portion of chicken in a horizontal row across the tortilla. Next, add a row of chutney (1 tablespoon). Next, a row of lettuce. Leave about 1½ inches of tortilla uncovered on one side. Sprinkle with about a tablespoon each of onion, cilantro, and bacon.

Roll up tightly, being careful not to tear. Gently pat the edge so that the herb cheese seals the roll, and wrap tightly in plastic wrap. Repeat with remaining tortillas and ingredients.

Refrigerate until ready to serve. Slice on the diagonal into 5 sections and arrange on a platter.

Serves 12

● ● ●

I'M CONFESSIN'

Dare to design your own wrap creations, but follow this one rule absolutely: layer ingredients so they can't get soggy. Don't place tomatoes, lettuce, or cucumbers directly against the flatbread or tortilla. Instead, start with a layer of fat—cheese or mayo, for instance— against the bread. Wraps are delicious as the flavors marry, so make them in advance, but banish wilt with this one simple rule.

SMOKED CHICKEN WRAPS WITH BACON, MANGO, AND RASPBERRY CHIPOTLE SAUCE

1 package of 6 large wraps or flour tortillas, flavored or plain
1 (8-ounce) container whipped cream cheese
2 cups smoked chicken, shredded
12 cooked bacon slices
1 ripe mango, cubed
3 green onions, chopped
½ cup chopped fresh mint
¼ cup raspberry chipotle sauce (or your favorite spicy barbecue sauce)

Spread 1 tortilla with about 2 tablespoons cream cheese, making sure the top edge is covered—this will be the "glue" that holds the wrap together.

Starting on the side closest to you, place ⅓ cup smoked chicken in a horizontal row across the tortilla. Next, add a row of mango. Leave about 1½ inches of tortilla uncovered on one side. Top with a generous sprinkle of bacon, green onions, and mint.

Drizzle with chipotle sauce. Roll up tightly, being careful not to tear. Gently pat the edge so that the cream cheese seals the roll, and wrap tightly in plastic wrap. Repeat with remaining tortillas and ingredients.

Refrigerate until ready to serve. Slice on the diagonal into 5 sections and arrange on a platter.

Serves 12

SMOKED SALMON AND BASIL WRAPS

1 package of 6 large wraps or flour tortillas, flavored or plain
1 (8-ounce) container whipped cream cheese
12 ounces smoked salmon, sliced
6 hard-cooked egg yolks, chopped
½ large red onion, finely chopped
6 teaspoons capers, drained
1 cup chopped ripe tomato, drained of excess juice
1 bunch basil, torn

Spread 1 tortilla with about 2 tablespoons cream cheese, making sure the top edge is covered—this will be the "glue" that holds the wrap together.

Starting on the side closest to you, place 2 ounces of salmon in a horizontal row across the tortilla. Next, add rows of egg yolks, chopped onion, capers, and tomato. Leave about 1½ inches of tortilla uncovered on one side. Sprinkle with basil.

Roll up tightly, being careful not to tear. Gently pat the edge so that the cream cheese seals the roll, and wrap tightly in plastic wrap. Repeat with remaining tortillas and ingredients.

Refrigerate until ready to serve. Slice on the diagonal into 5 sections and arrange on a platter.

Serves 12

GODDESSES OF GREEN

Raise the salad bar. Censure colorless iceberg and pale tomatoes—frisk the fridge for cheeses, veggies, and leftover bits of this or that. Stalk the pantry for nuts, dried fruit, beans, even a handful of those crunchy potato sticks (a staple on grocery shelves since 1935). Luxuriate in the tastes and textures of soft lettuce leaves folded with crunchy carrots, radishes, and sweet onion, then add a toss of toasted nuts, gooey cheese, olives, and perhaps a leftover chicken breast. Drizzle it all with a fabulous vinaigrette, and you've elevated greens to glorious main-course status. Whether it's the main event or a simple side with diva style, dare to create your own masterpiece. Don't despair over dinner— be green for a day.

• • • lush's LOVE-APPLE SALAD

The French first called tomatoes pommes d'amour, or "love apples," as they were considered aphrodisiacs. Perhaps they were right, for this easy-to-love, diva-licious salad always elicits smiles—and requests for seconds.

FOR THE SALAD:

2 large red, ripe tomatoes, cut into 8 wedges
2 large yellow, ripe tomatoes, cut into 8 wedges
1 cup halved grape tomatoes
6 large fresh basil leaves, rolled and thinly sliced
½ teaspoon coarse salt, or to taste
Cracked black pepper, to taste

FOR THE VINAIGRETTE

3 tablespoons balsamic vinegar
Salt and pepper, to taste
1 tablespoon Dijon mustard
1 tablespoon sugar
4 tablespoons extra-virgin olive oil

To prepare the salad, in a large bowl combine the tomatoes and basil; toss. Season with salt and pepper.

To prepare the vinaigrette, in a separate bowl season the balsamic vinegar with salt and pepper, then whisk in the mustard and sugar. Gradually add the oil and whisk until well mixed. Drizzle over the salad.

Serves 8

born to chop CHICKPEA SALAD

Abandon the vacuum, put on your pearls, and grab a cleaver, June. Just chop it and toss it—one bowl, one life, why spend it toiling in the kitchen? This salad is terrific with the Feta-Stuffed Lamb Burgers (page 124).

2 large ripe tomatoes, cored, seeded, and diced
2 cucumbers, peeled, seeded, and diced
½ small red onion, minced
1 garlic clove, minced
1 can chickpeas, rinsed and drained
2 tablespoons red wine vinegar
3 tablespoons extra-virgin olive oil
2 tablespoons fresh basil, chopped
2 tablespoons fresh flat-leaf parsley, minced
1 tablespoon fresh mint leaves, minced
½ cup pitted kalamata olives
Salt and pepper, to taste

In a large bowl, combine all ingredients then gently toss. Allow flavors to marry for about 15 minutes before serving. This salad can be made several hours ahead of time—just remember to remove from fridge about 20 minutes prior to serving.

Serves 8

• • •

I'M CONFESSIN'

Diligent divas can start with dried chickpeas that must be soaked and cooked, but can-do divas love this recipe—just open the can, give them a rinse, and these fiber-rich beauties are ready.

YOUR cheatin' HEART SALAD

• • •

I'M CONFESSIN'

Pantry princesses, these items, for the most part, should always be on your kitchen shelves. And there's room to play with this recipe: substitute any fresh herbs you love for the parsley. Use any tomatoes instead of grape; marinated artichokes could replace the hearts of palm.

Heart to heart, this couldn't be easier. So go on, it's OK to be sneaky: earn style points and cheat your way to gourmet salad success in five minutes flat. Silky, slender, ivory-colored hearts of palm are the edible inner portion of the cabbage palm tree, with flavor much like an artichoke. Dining alfresco? This cool, crunchy salad is splendor in the grass.

2 cans hearts of palm, cut diagonally into 1-inch lengths
1 cup halved grape tomatoes
2 celery ribs, thinly diagonally sliced
3 tablespoons minced fresh flat-leaf parsley, or more, to taste
2 tablespoons extra-virgin olive oil
1 tablespoon red wine vinegar, or more, to taste
Coarse salt and cracked black pepper to taste

Combine all ingredients in a large bowl; gently toss and serve chilled or at room temperature.

Serves 8

look-at-me MEDLEY WITH ASPARAGUS, CHOPPED EGG, and OLIVES

Step into the spotlight with this threesome. Broccoli can stand in for the asparagus, but be sure it's crisp-tender (save the mush for your man).

1 pound fresh asparagus, trimmed
3 hard-cooked eggs, chopped
1 cup pitted kalamata olives
1 recipe, Mama Lu's Mustard Vinaigrette (page 136)
Cracked black pepper, to taste

Parboil the asparagus for about 3 minutes or until crisp-tender; refresh in cold water. Divide onto 4 chilled plates, top evenly with the egg, then the pitted olives. Drizzle each portion with the vinaigrette, adding freshly ground pepper. This salad is also wonderful with grilled fish and chicken.

Serves 4

● ● ●

I'M CONFESSIN'

When you're short on time, the microwave can be your best friend. In a microwave-safe dish, place vegetables with about 1 tablespoon of water, salt and pepper, and a small drizzle of olive oil. Cover, then microwave on HIGH for four to five minutes. Remove the cover immediately so veggies won't continue to cook. And don't get burned: the steam trapped during cooking is definitely hot stuff.

I'M CONFESSIN'

Sexy, summer-fresh
fruit adds sizzle to
grilled fish, chicken,
or shrimp. Dress it up
with red onion, fresh
herbs, and even garlic
for fabulous salsas
and salads.

wild child WATERMELON, FETA, and MINT SALAD

Break out of your fruit rut and strut your stuff on the wild side. Salty feta, tart lime, and fresh mint transform watermelon to savory star status. No one can resist its summer charm, dressed to kill with a sprinkle of olive oil and cracked black pepper.

6 cups watermelon chunks, seeded
1 cup chopped feta cheese
¼ cup fresh mint, roughly chopped
Juice of 3 limes
4 tablespoons extra-virgin olive oil
Coarse salt and cracked black pepper, to taste

Combine the watermelon, feta, and chopped mint in a bowl. Drizzle in the lime juice and oil, tossing gently. Season with salt and pepper.

Serves 6

GARLIC harlot SALAD

Your healthy heart is hot to trot when fresh minced garlic adds sass to greens. Flush away cholesterol, demons, and ex-husbands with this garlic-infused Mediterranean meltdown stuffed with cheese, olives, nuts, and pepperoni. Dare to share with someone you love (bad breath be damned).

2 hearts (6 cups) of romaine lettuce, torn into bite-size pieces
½ cup julienned purple cabbage
1 cup chopped arugula
2 carrots, finely sliced or diced
½ medium onion, finely chopped
2 or 3 garlic cloves, minced
½ cup julienned turkey pepperoni
½ cup kasseri cheese, shredded
½ cup Spanish olives
½ cup chopped walnuts, toasted
Coarse salt and freshly ground pepper, to taste

Combine all ingredients in a large salad bowl; gently toss.

Serve with store-bought balsamic vinaigrette or a simple lemon vinaigrette. For a wonderful summer meal, add fresh-baked focaccia and slow-roasted tomatoes.

Serves 8

● ● ●

I'M CONFESSIN'

Will garlic really chase away vampires and bad hair days? Perhaps it is mere bad breath. Take the bite out of raw garlic by adding a sprinkle of coarse salt as you chop—makes it less pungent, while punching up the best of garlic's flavor. Or for those of you who prefer a milder garlic flavor, parboil your peeled cloves for about 1 minute.

I hate to gossip, but Lulu and I sometimes argue over how much cheese to use and what color the peppers should be, so play around with it. Fresh mozzarella has a soft texture and sweet, delicate flavor; buffalo mozzarella is the most prized, usually made from a combination of water buffalo and cow's milks. Lots of cracked black pepper adds contrast to both color and flavor.

VERNA'S voluptuous ORANGE PEPPER SALAD

Lusty, succulent bell peppers. Verna says go for buxom and bright—and don't scrimp on color. The more color, the more antioxidants—and the more antioxidants, the less wrinkles you'll get, which means you won't need to have a face-lift, which then means you won't be selfishly spending your children's college tuition money. Aging gracefully is in the bowl, babe.

2 orange or yellow or red bell peppers, coarsely chopped into bite-size pieces
1 cup fresh mozzarella, cut into bite-size pieces
3 tablespoons red wine vinegar
2 tablespoons extra-virgin olive oil
Coarse salt and cracked black pepper, to taste
¼ cup fresh torn basil or chopped parsley or 1 cup chopped fresh arugula

In a medium bowl, combine the peppers and the cheese; drizzle with the vinegar and oil and season with salt and pepper to taste. Toss gently with the fresh basil, parsley, or arugula. Serve immediately.

Serves 4

WASABI wallop CRUNCH

I'M CONFESSIN'

Any cheese will do (OK, no wrapped American slices). Experiment with your favorite nuts and salad greens.

Ever noticed how wasabi, the Japanese version of horseradish, gets you right in the nose? Oh, you'll feel the burn, honey. Crunchy wasabi peas (available in most grocery stores) are tossed right into this offbeat mélange, along with a variety of cheeses and nuts. Sweet grape tomatoes and a creamy dressing of your choice balance the punch of this sinus-scorching salad. Dinner is served.

3 to 4 cups romaine lettuce, washed, dried, and torn into bite-size pieces
Coarse salt and cracked black pepper, to taste
¼ cup shredded Parmesan cheese
¼ cup shredded baby Swiss cheese
2 tablespoons chopped walnuts
2 tablespoons pecans
2 tablespoons slivered almonds
¼ cup red onion, finely chopped
1 cup halved grape or cherry tomatoes, seasoned with salt and pepper
¼ cup wasabi peas

Combine all ingredients in a large bowl; mix with your favorite creamy dressing and serve.

Serves 4

cast off your caftan CUKES and 'MATERS SALAD

Dressing-room dread is a thing of the past: ban booty bloat and show off your teeny bikini with this thoroughly thigh-friendly fare. Cucumbers, along with other members of the melon family, flush away water weight—an unfortunate fact of life during the blazing days of summer. Chilly cukes and juicy 'maters make the scene with a splash of champagne vinegar and fresh dill. This taste-of-summer salad revolution really beats the heat. And you thought you had to exercise.

6 Kirby cucumbers, vertically halved and sliced
1 pint cherry tomatoes, rinsed and halved
½ small red onion, finely chopped
3 tablespoons minced fresh dill
3 to 4 tablespoons extra-virgin olive oil
2 tablespoons champagne vinegar
Coarse salt and cracked black pepper, to taste

Combine the first 4 ingredients in a large bowl; toss with the oil and vinegar. Season with salt and pepper.

Serves 8

● ● ●

I'M CONFESSIN'

Unashamed to show off? Toss in a few whole, roasted garlic cloves—it adds the diva dimension for gracious entertaining. Delicious and far less pungent than raw garlic, you can roast your own, or buy them ready to go in gourmet grocery stores.

There is a bit of work to making the warm vinaigrette, but don't despair: You can make it the day before. Just reheat before serving.

ooh, baby! SPINACH SALAD with CARAMELIZED ONION VINAIGRETTE

Long for love no more—your salad passion is finally sated. Chunks of crisp, smoky bacon gone to pieces, unsullied rounds of just-melting goat cheese, and tender baby spinach leaves reach a fever pitch nestled under a blanket of warm caramelized onion vinaigrette. Take your time as the tantalizing textures and flavors work their magic in your mouth.

½ **pound lean bacon, chopped**
2 **tablespoons olive oil**
2 **large sweet onions, sliced in half, then sliced into thin strips**
2 **tablespoons brown sugar**
4 **tablespoons balsamic vinegar, divided**
Coarse salt and cracked black pepper, to taste
½ **cup oil-packed sun-dried tomatoes, drained and chopped**
6 **cups baby spinach**
12 **ounces goat cheese, sliced into 8 rounds**

In a large skillet cook the bacon; drain on paper towels.

Wipe the skillet, leaving only a bit of the bacon fat. In the same pan over medium-high heat, add the olive oil and sauté the onions, adding the brown sugar and 1 tablespoon of the balsamic vinegar. Season with salt and pepper. The onions will slowly begin to caramelize; stir often so they don't burn. As the moisture evaporates, gradually add the rest of the balsamic vinegar. When the onions are completely caramelized (this should take about 30 minutes), taste and adjust the seasoning if necessary.

Add the sun-dried tomatoes and stir gently.

On 4 separate plates divide the baby spinach into equal portions, topping each with 2 rounds of the goat cheese. Crumble the reserved bacon over the cheese and top with the warm vinaigrette.

Serves 6

GET fresh WITH me SUMMER SALAD

Get fresh with a dilly summer favorite featuring kasseri, a Greek cheese made from sheep's or goat's milk with a sharp, salty flavor. This salad is perfect with any Greek entrée. You goat, girl!

1 bunch romaine lettuce, torn into bite-size pieces
2 tablespoons fresh dill, chopped
4 green onions, thinly diagonally sliced
½ cup shredded kasseri cheese
Juice of one lemon
½ teaspoon coarse salt
Cracked black pepper, to taste
2 tablespoons extra-virgin olive oil

In a salad bowl, toss the lettuce, dill, and green onions. Add the cheese and gently toss.

In a separate small bowl, whisk the lemon juice, salt, and pepper, then slowly add the olive oil, whisking until well blended. Drizzle over the salad, toss, and serve.

Serves 8

benevolent BEAN CURD SALAD

Tame the beast—pacify PMS. Iron-rich tofu, or soybean curd, is recommended to help balance haphazard hormones that fluctuate during certain times of the month. You're calm, cool, and collected when supple chunks of tofu, model-thin cuts of cucumber, and roasted sesame seeds save the day. And it comes together in a not-so-hot flash. So go ahead, treat yourself and the family with this dish that's low in calories, high in protein.

2 teaspoons honey
2 teaspoons rice vinegar
2 teaspoons toasted-sesame oil
6 teaspoons reduced-sodium soy sauce
¼ teaspoon crushed red pepper
8 ounces firm tofu, chopped into bite-size pieces
1 English cucumber, thinly sliced (if large, use half)
2 tablespoons toasted sesame seeds, for garnish

Combine first 5 ingredients in a bowl; whisk to incorporate.

In a separate bowl, toss the tofu and cucumber. Divide into equal portions on 4 serving plates, drizzle with the sauce, and sprinkle with sesame seeds. Serve with chopsticks.

Serves 4

● ● ●

I'M CONFESSIN'

Try this Asian dipping sauce (minus the tofu, cucumber, and sesame seeds) with steak, shrimp, or tossed with soba noodles.

FOREGONE fusion: FENNEL and ARUGULA

Assertive? Aromatic? We're talking about a salad that is loaded with style: a dynamic duo of aromatic fennel (the bulb is delicious raw) and the assertive bite of arugula dressed for success in a luscious lemon vinaigrette. Use fresh Parmesan here and save the canned stuff for the kiddies.

2 cups chopped fresh arugula
2 small fresh fennel bulbs
Juice of one lemon
½ teaspoon coarse salt
Freshly ground black pepper, to taste
4 tablespoons extra-virgin olive oil
¼ cup freshly grated Parmesan cheese

Chop the arugula until fragrant, then thinly slice the fennel. Toss together in a salad bowl.

In a small bowl, whisk together the lemon juice, salt, and pepper. Drizzle in the olive oil, whisking until well blended. Pour over the salad, toss with the Parmesan cheese, and serve immediately.

Serves 4

● ● ●

I'M CONFESSIN'

Twist and shout. Toss the ingredients for this versatile vinaigrette in a screw-top jar without measuring —just squeeze the lemon first, then add about 3 times the amount of your best olive oil. Seasoning the lemon juice before you add the oil makes for an easy emulsion. Shake it up, baby (just make sure the lid's on tight).

Roll tuna steaks in black sesame seeds (available in Asian grocery stores) for a nutty flavor and beautiful contrast with the color of the fish. Serve sashimi style with wasabi, pickled ginger, and soy sauce.

sayonara saddlebags
SEARED TUNA and GREENS

Do your thighs make you sigh? Toss out your granny panties and don your fishnets, divas. Just-seared yellowfin tuna is a super-buff source of low-fat protein that'll make you ooh, ahh, and beg for more. Add some dimple-defying vitamin-rich greens, and you can have this salad on the table in 10 short minutes. The lemon vinaigrette adds a decadent edge—but it will only seem that way since the extra-virgin olive oil is good for you, too.

Juice of 1 lemon
Coarse salt and freshly ground black pepper, to taste
4 tablespoons extra-virgin olive oil, divided
4 yellowfin tuna steaks (sushi grade)
1 package prewashed baby romaine lettuce leaves

In a small bowl, whisk together lemon juice, coarse salt, and pepper. Slowly drizzle in 2 tablespoons olive oil, whisking until well blended. Add salt and pepper to taste. Set aside.

Heat a nonstick pan and add 2 tablespoons of olive oil. Lightly season the tuna with salt and pepper. Sear in the pan about 1 minute on each side for medium rare (you can cook the tuna longer if you prefer it well done). Slice.

Divide the lettuce equally onto 4 plates and drizzle with the lemon vinaigrette. Top the greens with the tuna, drizzling each with a bit more of the vinaigrette, and add a flourish of freshly ground black pepper. Serve immediately.

Serves 4

sippin' señoritas SHRIMP SALAD with CHIPOTLE and AVOCADO

Pass the margaritas, señoritas! Make a big batch, as this spirited salad can pro-voke a powerful thirst. If the weather's nice, grab a blanket, invite your girlfriends, and gossip alfresco (we've always preferred spring fever to spring cleaning).

2 pounds cooked shrimp
4 green onions, sliced
4 garlic cloves, minced
2 ripe tomatoes, diced
2 jalapeño peppers, seeded and chopped
½ teaspoon ground cumin
½ teaspoon chipotle chile powder
½ teaspoon chili powder
1 cup frozen corn, thawed
1 cup canned black beans, rinsed and drained
3 tablespoons minced fresh cilantro
1 teaspoon hot sauce
Coarse salt and cracked black pepper, to taste
Juice of 2 limes
3 to 4 tablespoons extra-virgin olive oil
4 Hass avocados, skinned, halved , and pitted
Fresh cilantro (optional)
Sour cream (optional)

In a large bowl, combine the first 15 ingredients. Chill for 30 minutes to 1 hour, then serve mounded on avocado halves. Garnish with extra cilantro and sour cream if desired.

Serves 10

• • •

I'M CONFESSIN'

Girls just wanna have fun; peeling and deveining shrimp is not. Flash-frozen shrimp that's ready to cook not only makes life easier, but it also often tastes better than that sold as fresh. Thaw it quickly under cold, running water.

my BIG, fat GREEK CHICKEN SALAD

Spread your apron strings and fly the coop; escape the ordinary ladies-who-lunch chicken-and-mayo medley. Our big, fat chicken salad is a welcome twist on an old standard. With piquant, sweet and savory flavors, this diva-licious main-course salad comes together quickly with just a knife, cutting board, and bowl. Verna and Lulu serve with crackers or pita bread. Greek olives (and Greek gods, for that matter) are fabulous on the side. Live it up.

6 cups roasted chicken breast, torn or chopped into bite-size pieces
1 cup crumbled feta cheese
½ red onion, finely chopped
6 ounces oil-packed sun-dried tomatoes, drained
3 or 4 garlic cloves, minced
½ cup mayonnaise
1 teaspoon dried oregano
Juice of ½ lemon
2 tablespoons chopped fresh mint
Coarse salt and cracked black pepper, to taste

Combine all ingredients in a large bowl, tossing together gently—you can even use your hands for this. Chill for at least 1 hour before serving. The salad can be made several hours in advance, or even the day prior to serving. Before serving, check seasoning. You may want to add extra lemon juice or a few turns of freshly ground black pepper. And if you make it in advance, fold in the fresh mint just before serving.

Serves 8 to 10

thai-me-up CAESAR SALAD with SMOKED CHICKEN

Feed your Caesar salad fantasies and get kinky with a classic beauty. Smoked chicken and tender, leafy greens keep your love alive, while fish sauce, popular throughout Southeast Asia, plays a double role, providing both the salt and anchovy flavors of classic Caesar dressing. To keep things fresh, use only your best-quality olive oil and minced, fresh garlic.

2 tablespoons fish sauce
1 tablespoon fresh lemon juice
4 garlic cloves , minced
Cracked black pepper, to taste
3 tablespoons extra-virgin olive oil
4 cups romaine lettuce, torn into bite-size pieces
2 cups prepared smoked chicken
¼ cup shaved Parmesan cheese

Combine the fish sauce, lemon juice, garlic, and cracked pepper. Whisk in the olive oil until well blended.

In a salad bowl, combine the lettuce and chicken, then toss with the vinaigrette. Top with Parmesan cheese.

Serves 6

• • •

I'M CONFESSIN'

Get caught in curlers: for beautiful curls of shaved Parmesan, use your vegetable peeler. If you can't find smoked chicken, substitute smoked turkey—or leave out the meat entirely and just go for the green.

Like a seductive shade of lipstick or girl-next-door pearls, side dishes can give your main course diva sizzle, transforming "a little something on the side" to sensational.

Side dishes can have more wow power than a main dish, but always try to balance the flavors: buttery Chilean sea bass pairs well with something slightly acidic, such as thick-cut, perfectly ripened tomato slices drizzled with an easy lemon vinaigrette.

Color, too, plays a starring role. You can give an unadorned menu a makeover with something as easy as a toss of fresh green herbs or a few curls of lemon zest. Or, with a nod to the official color wheel, consider these natural beauties: braised purple cabbage with golden,

DES

roasted butternut squash, or lightly cooked baby spinach and caramelized tomatoes. And there's a bonus because this rainbow of colors is the best way to get a range of nutrients.

You glow, girl—but the hostess with the mostest never lets 'em see her sweat. For dinner parties, choose sides that work in your time frame and won't keep you from your company. If your main course is over the top, think simple—or be a do-ahead diva and go for something you can make in advance and quickly reheat.

Or resign yourself to room temperature: entertaining will never be easier, and there are plenty of dishes that taste delicious in the temperate zone. Now that's using your noodle.

grab your girdle GARLIC SMASHED TATERS

Like bobby pins in a beehive hairstyle, you can never have too much butter in smashed potatoes. For the most creamy, dreamy spuds, go ahead and butter 'em up . . . the bowl will be empty before your lipstick wears off. And just this once, calories be damned. If you like the potato skins, you can leave them on.

6 medium Yukon gold potatoes, cut into 1-inch cubes
10 to 15 garlic cloves, peeled
Coarse salt and cracked black pepper, to taste
6 tablespoons unsalted butter
¼ cup heavy cream

Peel the potatoes and dice into 1-inch pieces.

Place the potatoes in a medium stockpot. Cover the potatoes with water and season with salt and pepper. Add the garlic cloves and simmer for 20 minutes or until the potatoes are very tender. Drain the water from the pot and return the pot to the stove over low heat.

Shake the potatoes, allowing the excess water to steam away. When the potatoes begin to whiten around the edges, remove from heat.

With a potato masher, mash the potatoes and soft garlic cloves together. Add the butter and cream, stirring vigorously until slightly smooth, allowing some of the chunky potato texture to remain. Season to taste with salt and pepper.

Serves 8

... they did the LOBSTER MASH

I'M CONFESSIN'

Divas, this is death by demi-glace, so don't be tempted to skip the seemingly arduous process of reducing the lobster stock. If you can boil water, you're in the pink.

This voluptuous pairing of buttery, silken potatoes and chunks of lobster is over the top, but, oh, your dinner guests never had it so good. The divas indulged and lived to create their own sinful version, inspired by a chef at Disney's California Grill. Serve it with simple grilled fish and a green salad—this side is the star of the show. The demi-glace can be prepared up to a week in advance.

FOR THE DEMI-GLACE:

6 cups water
1 cup chicken stock
½ cup dry white wine
2 celery ribs, chopped
½ medium onion, sliced
2 carrots, chopped
2 tablespoons chopped fresh parsley
1 bay leaf
Salt and pepper, to taste
2 lobster tails

FOR THE MASHED POTATOES:

4 large baking potatoes, peeled and chopped
4 garlic cloves, peeled
6 tablespoons unsalted butter
4 tablespoons heavy cream
1 cup pasteurized lobster meat

To prepare the demi-glace, combine the water, stock, wine, celery, onion, carrots, parsley, and bay leaf; season with salt and pepper. Bring to a gentle simmer, then add the lobster tails.

Cook the tails until just opaque, then remove and allow them to cool. Remove the tail meat and set aside (refrigerate if you are making the demi-glace ahead of time).

Return the shells to the stock and turn up the heat. Boil for 1 hour, then strain to remove the shells and vegetables.

Place the strained stock back on the stove and reduce for about another hour. As the lobster stock begins to thicken, reduce the heat to medium-low and stir often until it is thick enough to coat the back of a spoon. This demi-glace can be stored in the refrigerator until ready to use.

To prepare the mashed potatoes, place the potatoes in a large stockpot. Cover the potatoes with water and season with salt and pepper. Add the garlic cloves and simmer for 20 minutes or until the potatoes are very tender. Drain the water from the pot and return the pot to the stove over low heat. Shake the potatoes, allowing the excess water to steam away. When the potatoes begin to whiten around the edges, remove from heat.

In the same pan, mash the potatoes and garlic with a potato masher; add the butter, cream, and lobster demi-glace. Taste and adjust the seasoning if necessary. Cut the lobster tail meat and the pasteurized lobster meat into chunks, and gently warm. Fold into the potatoes and serve.

Serves 6

star-style SCALLOPED POTATOES

There's nothing half-baked about this swanky version of old-fashioned scalloped potatoes. Comforting chunks of buttery Yukon gold potatoes have a starring role, mixed with smoky bits of bacon, melted cheese, and bursts of robust sun-dried tomatoes. Go ahead—tight pants (and big hair) are always in vogue.

1 pound Yukon gold potatoes, cut into ¼-inch slices
Coarse salt and cracked black pepper, to taste
1 cup shredded sharp Cheddar cheese
¼ cup torn fresh basil
¼ cup oil-packed sun-dried tomatoes, drained and chopped
4 to 6 slices bacon, cooked and crumbled
¾ cup chicken stock or broth
3 garlic cloves, minced

Preheat oven to 350°.

Place the potatoes in a large stockpot. Cover the potatoes with water and boil until just tender. Drain and season with salt and pepper.

In a 13 x 9–inch baking dish, layer the potatoes with the cheese, basil, sun-dried tomatoes, and bacon. (If using a smaller dish, you can make several layers.)

Pour the chicken stock over the potatoes; sprinkle with garlic and bake at 350° for 20 minutes or until the potatoes are completely tender and the cheese is melted. Garnish with extra basil if desired.

Serves 8

booty-licious BLACK BEANS

Need we say more? Go for booty and brains: serve this savory side with roast pork, picadillo, or fish. Or shake your booty center stage with whole-grain tortillas, chopped fresh herbs, avocado, tomato, and goat cheese. High in protein and fiber, it's good for your health. Bottoms up!

1 small onion, chopped
½ green pepper, chopped
2 to 3 garlic cloves, minced
2 tablespoons extra-virgin olive oil
Coarse salt and cracked black pepper, to taste
½ teaspoon ground cumin
½ teaspoon dried oregano
1 bay leaf
1 teaspoon hot sauce (optional)
1 teaspoon minced fresh cilantro
2 (14.5-ounce) cans black beans, rinsed and drained
½ cup dry white wine
½ cup chicken stock

In a 2½-quart saucepan over medium-high heat, sauté the onion, pepper, and garlic in the olive oil. Season with salt and pepper, cumin, oregano, and bay leaf. Add the hot sauce if desired; add cilantro.

As the vegetables begin to soften, add the beans, wine, and stock. Simmer, uncovered, for 20 minutes, stirring occasionally. Remove the bay leaf.

Serves 6

• • •

I'M CONFESSIN'

Girlfriends, you know how important it is to eat plenty of fiber-rich foods. Not to be indelicate, but Verna certainly knows what happens to me when I do not. Black beans contain up to 6 grams of fiber in a mere half-cup. And pantry-perfect canned varieties make it easy to, um, keep things running smoothly. Look for beans that are not pre-seasoned.

japanese NOODLE nosh

• • •

I'M CONFESSIN'

Earn style points by serving this noodle bowl with chopsticks, fresh basil and cilantro, and chopped peanuts. If you're a naughty hottie, add a dollop of chile garlic sauce (available in Asian grocery stores and many supermarkets) to spice things up. Oh, and calories consumed after 10 p.m. do not affect your waistline— this is a fabulous late-night nosh.

Throw together this make-ahead side that proves opposites really do attract—a splash of vinegar and a spoonful of honey create the perfect yin-yang. Expect some undiva-like slurping at the table as your guests enjoy the combination of chewy noodles and crispy cucumbers.

¼ cup sesame seeds
2 teaspoons rice vinegar
2 teaspoons sesame oil
6 teaspoons soy sauce
2 teaspoons honey
8 ounces noodles of your choice (lo mein, soba, whole wheat)
4 green onions, thinly diagonally sliced
1 lime, quartered
Seedless cucumber, julienned for garnish (optional)

Toast the sesame seeds in a nonstick skillet, shaking often, until golden; remove from heat and set aside.

Whisk together the vinegar, sesame oil, soy sauce, and honey.

Cook the noodles according to package directions; drain and rinse in cold water. Shake the colander to remove excess water, and place the noodles in a serving bowl. Toss with the sauce and green onions. Add the sesame seeds and toss again, then add a generous squeeze of lime juice. Chill for at least an hour to allow flavors to mingle.

Taste and adjust the seasoning if necessary—an extra dash of soy sauce livens the taste. Garnish with cucumber if desired. Serve cold.

Serves 6

forbidden RICE MEDLEY

Here's the dish: an exotic, nutty, onyx-colored rice bejeweled with colorful veggies, tossed with a tangy vinaigrette, then chilled to perfection. Perfect for an alfresco summer buffet or as a do-ahead, healthful picnic or potluck item. Only the name is forbidden.

FOR THE VINAIGRETTE:
2 tablespoons red wine vinegar
1 tablespoon sugar
½ teaspoon coarse salt
1 teaspoon Dijon mustard
4 tablespoons extra-virgin olive oil
Cracked black pepper, to taste

FOR THE SALAD:
1 cup forbidden or black rice, thoroughly rinsed
2 cups cold water
½ red bell pepper, diced
¼ red onion, finely chopped
¾ cup frozen corn, thawed
½ seedless cucumber, peeled and chopped
½ cup golden raisins

To prepare the vinaigrette, in a small bowl whisk together the first 6 ingredients. Set aside.

Combine rice and 2 cups cold water in a saucepan. Bring to a vigorous boil, then turn heat to low and cover with a tight-fitting lid. Continue cooking until all water is absorbed, about 15 minutes. Remove from heat and let stand, covered, for 10 minutes. Cool.

In a large bowl toss together the bell pepper, red onion, corn, cucumbers, and raisins. Add the black rice, then stir in the vinaigrette. Chill for at least 3 hours or overnight. Taste and adjust the seasoning if necessary.

Serves 10

put me on a pedestal
PURPLE CABBAGE

Just wear sensible shoes. You'll tower over the competition with this gorgeous, creamy taste sensation. We especially love this sassy cabbage with pork tenderloin.

½ cup walnuts, toasted
2 tablespoons extra-virgin olive oil
½ head purple cabbage, thinly sliced
Coarse salt and cracked black pepper, to taste
2 tablespoons balsamic vinegar
1 tablespoon dark brown sugar
½ cup crumbled goat cheese

Toast the walnuts in a nonstick skillet until slightly browned and fragrant (about 5 minutes), stirring often; set aside.

In a large nonstick skillet, heat the oil and add the cabbage; season with salt and pepper. Add the balsamic vinegar and brown sugar and sauté over medium-high heat until just crisp-tender, about 5 minutes.

Remove from heat; toss with cheese and nuts.

Serves 4

• • •
I'M CONFESSIN'

Color them hungry. It's not just psycho-babble—colors evoke powerful emotions. Adding more color to your plate adds "diva drama" while keeping you healthy and (most importantly) looking fine. Serve this dish with ripe yellow tomatoes garnished with your favorite fresh herbs.

mamacita's CALABACITAS

To the chopping challenged, forget about seeding the bell pepper. Instead, hold the pepper upright, and make downward vertical cuts where the pepper is convex. Next, flip the pepper upside down, and cut off the bottom. You will cut away the usable portion of the pepper without having to deal with the seeds or pithy ribs.

Love me slender. Calabacitas is a simple sauté of fresh veggies that is muy sabroso. *South of the border sizzle with gorgeous color, mucho flavor, and very little fat. Serve on the side or as a vegetarian main course folded into whole-grain tortillas.*

2 medium zucchini, cut into ¼-inch-thick slices
2 yellow summer squash, cut into ¼-inch-thick slices
1 red bell pepper, seeded and cut into strips
1 small Vidalia or other sweet onion, sliced
2 ears corn, kernels removed
2 tablespoons extra-virgin olive oil
Salt and freshly ground black pepper, to taste
½ teaspoon ground cumin
Juice of 1 lime
¼ cup shredded sharp Cheddar cheese

In a large nonstick skillet over high heat, sauté the vegetables in the oil until just crisp-tender, about 5 minutes. Season with salt, pepper, and cumin. Sprinkle with lime juice and serve immediately with the shredded cheese.

Serves 8

go slow SWEET ROASTED TOMATOES

Patience is a virtue, but you'll be longing for these tomatoes as they slowly roast.
Please me, don't tease me—then it's love at first bite (men are so overrated).

2 pounds plum tomatoes or a mixture of vine ripe red and yellow tomatoes
6 tablespoons extra-virgin olive oil
Coarse salt and cracked black pepper, to taste
Balsamic glaze, approximately ¼ cup (available in specialty gourmet shops)
Fresh torn basil, to taste

Preheat oven to 300°.

Slice the tomatoes in half; arrange cut sides up on a baking sheet or shallow baking pan. Drizzle olive oil over each tomato, then season with salt and pepper.

Roast for about 3 hours (start checking at 2 ½ hours if your oven is extra-hot). You want the tomatoes to be caramelized, not blackened. Remove from oven; drizzle with the glaze and sprinkle with basil. The tomatoes can be served warm or at room temperature.

Serves 12

I'M CONFESSIN'

OK, diva wannabes, this is our little secret: you can use tomatoes that aren't quite perfect because the roasting concentrates their flavor. For oh-so-elegant entertaining, use both yellow and red tomatoes. A drizzle of dark balsamic glaze contrasts beautifully with the color of the tomatoes and fresh torn basil leaves.

If you can't find bottled balsamic glaze, it's easy to make. Combine 1 cup balsamic vinegar with 3 tablespoons brown sugar, and simmer for 30 minutes until nicely thickened (your glaze will continue to thicken as it cools). To decorate like a pro, put the balsamic glaze in a squeeze bottle.

SOUPER

Faster than a speeding can opener, more powerful than a rotten cold! Able to leap tall kitchen counters in a single bound. Look! Up in the sky. It's a bird. It's a plane. It's Souper Diva! Strange visitor from another planet who came to your kitchen with powers and abilities far beyond those of mortal housewives. Who can change the course of picky eaters. Who can incorporate all food groups in a single pot with her bare hands. Who says "I love you" or "Feel better" more compellingly than any card or bouquet. And who, disguised as "Mom," a mild-mannered (if hormonally challenged) chef, fights for all leftovers; healthful, economical choices; and fabulous flavor for the great American soup pot.

You, too, can feel just like Souperwoman when you offer up a bubbly, soul-infused bowl of homemade goodness.

DIVA!

Purists start from scratch, crafting stocks and soaking beans overnight. Busy cooks can take the easy way out with leftovers from a roasted chicken, a judicious squeeze of fresh lemons, dried noodles, a toss of fresh herbs, and a can of broth from a well-stocked pantry. Given the harrowing pace of balancing work and family, convenience, and, well, sanity, most of these simple recipes embrace ease.

Be serendipitous and substitute with what you have on hand—even leftovers du jour—for our ingredients. Or pour a glass of wine and spend a rainy afternoon concocting a simmering soup masterpiece. Freeze half, then joyously devour the remainder some busy evening when cooking seems beyond all reason.

I'M CONFESSIN'

A trio of tips: Fines herbes is a savory mix of dried, finely chopped herbs, usually chervil, chives, parsley, and tarragon. You'll find it on most grocery store shelves.

We couldn't live without our inexpensive, portable immersion blender: just plunge one right in the pot of soup and pulsate your way to mess-free, one-pot pureeing.

White beans are a wonderful base for just about any veggie soup. Toss in your own inspirations —say, from cleaning out the refrigerator. Fresh zucchini, summer squash, and spinach all work well in this soup.

under the TUSCAN sun WHITE BEAN SOUP

What's for dinner, Verna? Summon the robust flavors of Tuscany without leaving the cul-de-sac. Thick, rich, quick, and yummy, tantalize your tummy with a blend of fresh onions, celery, carrots, and tender cannellini beans. (I'll bring the wine.)

½ large onion, chopped
2 celery ribs, chopped
2 carrots, peeled and sliced
3 tablespoons extra-virgin olive oil, divided
Coarse salt and cracked black pepper, to taste
3 garlic cloves, minced
¼ cup chopped fresh parsley, divided
1 teaspoon fines herbes (or a mixture of chervil, tarragon, and basil)
1 bay leaf
3 cups chicken stock
1 cup white wine
1 large potato, peeled and diced
2 (14.5-ounce) cans cannellini beans, drained
Juice of ½ lemon
Lemon wedges (optional)

In a stockpot over medium-low heat, sauté the onion, celery, and carrots in olive oil. Season with salt and pepper.

As the vegetables begin to soften, add the garlic and 2 tablespoons fresh parsley, the fines herbes, and the bay leaf. Sauté carefully, stirring often so as not to brown the garlic, about 2 minutes.

Add the chicken stock, wine, and diced potato. Bring to a simmer and cook for 10 minutes.

Add the cannellini beans. Cover and simmer for 30 minutes or until the potatoes are tender.

Allow the soup to cool slightly and discard the bay leaf. Ladle half of the soup into a blender or food processor; puree and return this portion to the pot. Or use an immersion blender to partially puree the soup, leaving a slightly chunky texture.

Add the lemon juice, olive oil, and the remaining fresh parsley. Taste and adjust the seasoning if necessary.

Serve with lemon wedges if desired.

Serves 8

creamy, dreamy CHOWDER

I'M CONFESSIN'

Don't go against the grain: fresh corn is a wonderful source of fiber. Stewing the cobs in the stock extracts every delicious bit of fresh corn flavor. Garnish with fresh lime wedges and sour cream, if ya wanna.

A hale and hearty, man-pleasin', taste bud–teasin' stew of roasted chiles, smoky bacon, and fresh corn is a crowd pleaser every time.

1 large poblano chile
6 slices turkey bacon, chopped
1 medium onion, chopped
2 tablespoons olive oil
1 carrot, thinly sliced
4 garlic cloves, minced
1 teaspoon dried oregano, preferably Mexican
½ teaspoon ground cumin
1 teaspoon ground coriander
¼ teaspoon cayenne pepper
Coarse salt and cracked black pepper, to taste
6 ears fresh corn, kernels removed, reserving 2 of the cobs
1 large potato, peeled and diced
6 cups chicken stock
1 cup white wine
2 corn tortillas, sliced
Juice of 2 limes
Juice of ½ lemon
2 tablespoons unsalted butter
¼ cup minced fresh cilantro

Preheat the broiler. Roast the poblano chile until the skin is charred. Cool in a paper bag and then slip the skin off. Chop and set aside.

In a large stockpot, sauté the turkey bacon and onion in olive oil. Add the carrot, garlic, and spices, stirring, careful not to burn the garlic. Season with salt and pepper to taste.

Add the corn and two corncobs (for flavor), diced potato, stock, wine, and tortillas. Bring to a simmer; cover and cook for 30 minutes, stirring occasionally. Taste and adjust seasoning if necessary. Add the chopped poblano.

Remove the corncobs. With an immersion blender or conventional blender, puree the soup in batches, returning the pureed soup to the pot. Simmer over low heat for 5 minutes. Stir in the lime and lemon juice, butter, and fresh cilantro.

Serves 8

macho GAZPACHO

Real men eat gazpacho: lusty red, ripe tomatoes; crisp cucumbers; and the peppery zest of chopped arugula gone wild. Chill out with this garden of earthly delights zapped with a burst of fresh lime and a drop or two of heat.

FOR THE SOUP:

6 ripe beefsteak tomatoes, chopped
1 small sweet onion, chopped
1 English cucumber, peeled and chopped
2 garlic cloves
2 slices stale French bread
1 cup arugula, roughly chopped
2 tablespoons extra-virgin olive oil
Juice of ½ lime
1 teaspoon hot sauce (optional)
1 tablespoon red wine vinegar
¾ cup tomato juice (or a 6-ounce can)
Coarse salt and cracked black pepper, to taste
2 tablespoons extra-virgin olive oil

GARNISHES:

2 cups chopped cucumber
3 Hass avocados, peeled and chopped
¼ cup chopped cilantro, mint, or parsley
Sour cream
1 cup chopped green olives

Combine the first 6 ingredients in a blender and puree. Stir in the remaining ingredients; taste and adjust the seasoning if necessary. Chill for at least 2 hours.

Serve with the garnishes if desired.

Serves 8

I'M CONFESSIN'

On a warm summer's evening, serve this chilled soup with a dollop of fresh crab-meat or chilled shrimp for a lusciously light meal.

This is a great recipe to create with the children in your life, be they sons, daughters, nieces, nephews, or grandchildren. Cooking opens a whole new world to kids. It builds relationships, develops a sense of teamwork, and is just plain fun. And though it may take a bit more time to get dinner on the table, creative kitchen play is a lifetime memory for little ones.

little PURSES in GINGER BROTH

Indulge your passion for (food) fashion in style: to-die-for designer dumplings filled with savory garlic chicken nestled in a light, gingery broth.

FOR THE DUMPLINGS:

1 pound ground chicken
2 tablespoons soy sauce
1 tablespoon fresh ginger, minced
1 tablespoon fresh garlic, minced
2 teaspoons dry sherry
3 green onions, chopped
1 egg white
2 teaspoons sesame oil
1 teaspoon sugar
1 teaspoon cornstarch
About 40 wonton wrappers

FOR THE GINGER BROTH:

8 cups chicken stock
1 (2-inch) piece fresh ginger, sliced
4 tablespoons soy sauce
2 green onions, chopped
4 tablespoons matchstick-cut carrots
Green onions or cilantro (optional)

To prepare the dumplings, in a large bowl thoroughly mix the first 10 ingredients. (Make these with the kids—they love to get their hands messy.)

Clear a work surface and fill a small bowl with water. Use a lightly dampened towel to cover the completed wontons as you go, as the dough dries out quickly.

Lay a wonton wrapper flat and place a small spoonful of the filling in the center. With your fingers or a small brush, moisten the edges of the wonton wrapper. Fold the edges up over the filling, creating a small "purse." Squeeze together at the top to seal, being careful not to rip the fragile dough. Repeat with the remaining filling and wontons, placing the finished dumplings on a plate and covering with a damp towel.

To prepare the ginger broth, heat the stock in a large pot, adding the ginger. Simmer for 10 minutes, remove the ginger, then add soy sauce, green onions, and carrots.

With a large slotted spoon, carefully add the dumplings. They will float to the surface when cooked through (about 3 minutes). Do not overcook. Serve in petite Asian bowls; garnish with extra green onions or cilantro if desired.

Serves 8

I'M CONFESSIN'

I like to pour some of the dipping sauce right into my bowl, though the proper way to do this is to dip the noodles and chicken as you go. Perhaps the most brilliant aspect of this fabulous soup is that it is at once as simple —or as complex—as you need it to be. My son, the purist, prefers a simple bowl with lots of noodles, whereas Verna and I positively lavish ours with herbs, sprouts, lime, and garlic chile paste.

UN-pho-GETTABLE PHO GA vietnamese CHICKEN NOODLE SOUP

You never "pho-get" your first bowl. Oodles of soft, silken noodles adrift in a gingery bowl of comfort-infused broth. You could stop right there and be well on your way to boundless, soup-slurping bliss, but why not pile on some fresh, sweet basil leaves, a sprightly toss of crunchy bean sprouts, and a refreshing drizzle of lime juice?

FOR THE DIPPING SAUCE:

2 garlic cloves, minced
1 hot red chile, seeded and finely sliced
1 (1½ -inch) piece fresh ginger, peeled and finely minced
3 tablespoons fish sauce
Juice of 1 lime
5 tablespoons water
2 tablespoons sugar

FOR THE SOUP:

8 cups chicken broth
1 (2-inch) piece fresh ginger, sliced
2 cinnamon sticks
1 pound rice vermicelli or thin egg noodles
4 tablespoons soy sauce
2 tablespoons rice vinegar
1 tablespoon sesame oil
½ cup grated carrot
2 skinless, boneless chicken breasts
3 green onions, thinly sliced

GARNISHES:

2 limes, quartered
Several sprigs fresh cilantro
Several sprigs fresh basil
2 cups bean sprouts
2 red chiles, seeded and sliced
Garlic chile paste, to taste

To prepare the dipping sauce, combine the first 7 ingredients in a bowl. Whisk and set aside.

To prepare the soup, in a stockpot bring the chicken broth to a boil and add the ginger and cinnamon. Reduce the heat and simmer for 10 minutes.

While the broth simmers, in a separate pan prepare the noodles al dente according to the package directions; drain, rinse with cold water and set aside.

With a slotted spoon, remove the ginger slices and cinnamon sticks from the broth. Add the soy sauce, vinegar, sesame oil, and carrot.

With a sharp knife, slice the chicken breasts as thinly as possible (no more than ¼-inch thick). Add the chicken and cook in the broth until opaque, about 3 minutes. The broth should be at a nice simmer, not a vigorous boil, as that will toughen the chicken. Toss in the green onions and give them a stir.

To serve, spoon the noodles into bowls and then cover them with the broth. Garnish if desired. Arrange the limes, herbs, sprouts, and chiles on a platter and serve with the soup, dipping sauce, and garlic chile paste.

Serves 6

all better CHICKEN SOUP with CHERVIL and FRESH LEMON JUICE

Mmm, mmm good. You could open a can … but why would you? Perhaps nothing says "I love you" more eloquently than a fragrant bowl of homemade chicken soup. Breathe in the love; banish a nasty cold, open hearts and sinuses.

3 tablespoons olive oil
1 medium onion, chopped
4 celery ribs, chopped
4 carrots, peeled and chopped
2 tablespoons fresh minced parsley
Coarse salt and cracked black pepper, to taste
1 teaspoon fines herbes
1 teaspoon chervil
2 or 3 skinless, bone-in chicken breast halves
6 cups chicken stock or broth
1 cup dry white wine
8 ounces wide egg noodles, or 1 cup orzo
Juice of 1 lemon
Fresh parsley (optional)

In a large soup pot over medium-low heat, heat the oil and add the onion, celery, carrots, and fresh parsley, seasoning with salt and pepper. Sprinkle the vegetable mixture with the fines herbes and chervil.

When the vegetables are tender and fragrant, add the chicken, seasoning the breasts with salt and pepper. Pour in the stock and wine. Cover and simmer for 20 to 30 minutes, or until the chicken is tender to slide easily off the bone.

Remove the chicken (and any bones) from the pot; cool. Remove the meat from the bones; tear the meat into bite-size pieces.

Meanwhile, add the noodles to the broth and vegetable mixture. Simmer until the noodles are tender; turn off the heat and add the chicken pieces.

Add the lemon juice and adjust seasoning if necessary. Garnish with additional fresh parsley if desired.

Serves 10

TORTILLA mia SOUP

I'M CONFESSIN'

To each his own. Tortilla soup is a Tex-Mex staple that invites individuality, from the most basic bowl of comfort-infused broth to a culinary master-piece of flavors and textures. Serve with a buffet of fresh herbs, chopped avocado, chiles, olives, cubed chicken, and crunchy tortilla chips.

2 tablespoons olive oil
1 large sweet onion, chopped
6 corn tortillas, cut into pieces
Coarse salt and cracked black pepper, to taste
4 garlic cloves, chopped
8 cups chicken stock
3 skinless, boneless chicken breasts
Juice of 2 lemons
Juice of 4 limes

GARNISHES:

2 Hass avocados, peeled and chopped
1 bunch cilantro, chopped
2 jalapeño peppers, seeded and finely chopped
4 or 5 plum tomatoes, seeded and chopped
Tortilla chips
Shredded cheeses of your choice
Sliced black olives
Sour cream
Salsa

In a large soup pot, heat the oil. Add the onions and tortilla pieces; season with salt and pepper. Sauté until the onion is translucent and fragrant. Add the chopped garlic and cook for 1 minute.

Pour in the stock. Bring to a simmer and add the chicken breasts. Poach breasts for about 10 minutes. Remove the chicken from the pot and allow to cool.

With an immersion blender, puree the stock mixture, or use your regular blender and then return mixture to the pot. Simmer the broth another 15 minutes, uncovered, allowing to thicken slightly.

Meanwhile, chop or slice the chicken. (You can add the chicken back to the soup, or use it as a garnish.)

Remove the soup from the heat and add the lemon and lime juice, adjusting seasoning if necessary. Ladle the broth into bowls and let everyone add their own garnishes.

Serves 10

quickie in the kitchen
CHICKEN STEW

Better not tell the butler: the upstairs maid can't resist this quickie bistro concoction of tender chicken, prosciutto, new potatoes, and fresh herbs. As it seductively simmers on the stovetop, fragrant tendrils of yum beckon. Pour the wine, break the bread—give in to passion one spoonful at a time.

3 tablespoons extra-virgin olive oil, divided
2 large leeks, cleaned and thinly diagonally sliced
2 garlic cloves, minced
1 carrot, thinly sliced
4 tablespoons chopped fresh flat-leaf parsley, divided
Coarse salt and cracked black pepper, to taste
4 or 5 thin slices prosciutto, roughly chopped
1 pound chicken tenderloins
8 small new potatoes, quartered
2 (14-ounce) cans chicken broth
⅓ cup dry white wine
Juice of ½ lemon
2 tablespoons chopped fresh mint
1 tablespoon torn fresh basil

Heat 2 tablespoons of olive oil in a stockpot over medium-high heat. Sauté the leeks, garlic, carrot, and 3 tablespoons of fresh parsley. Season lightly with salt and pepper.

Sauté the vegetables until tender. Add the prosciutto, chicken, potatoes, broth, and wine; bring to a simmer.

Cover the pot, reducing heat to medium-low. Allow to simmer 25 minutes or until potatoes are tender, stirring occasionally.

Remove from heat; add remaining tablespoon of olive oil, remaining tablespoon of chopped fresh parsley, lemon juice, fresh mint, and basil.

Serves 8

● ● ●

I'M CONFESSIN'

Don't be bashful: play around with our ingredients to make this soup your own. Substitute Italian sausage for the prosciutto, or fresh tarragon for the basil or mint. And remember, a bit of acidity (such as fresh lemon juice) added at the end of cooking time will balance the flavors.

POT o' simmerin' love
ITALIAN CHICKEN STEW

Salt and pepper are
such personal pref-
erences, we keep a
small bowl of kosher
salt by the stove and
season as we go.
Divas love breaking
rules, so we usually
ignore amounts of
salt and pepper in any
recipe and season to
our own taste. Just re-
member, when "build-
ing" a soup, season as
you go. Just a pinch
of salt with the onions
as they cook, an-
other for subsequent
veggies as they are
added—even water
needs to be seasoned.
To prevent oversalt-
ing, use your fingers
to sprinkle, and taste
frequently, just like the
culinary pros.

When the moon hits your eye like a big pizza pie, that's amore. Then again, a fragrant bowl of this luscious stew might just do the trick. Aromatherapy must have originated in Italy: sun-ripened tomatoes, onions, peppers, and fresh herbs bubbling together with a lavish pour of fruity olive oil.

2 tablespoons extra-virgin olive oil
1 small onion, chopped
1 small red bell pepper, chopped
2 celery ribs, chopped
Coarse salt and cracked black pepper, to taste
6 garlic cloves, minced
1 teaspoon dried oregano
1 teaspoon dried basil
½ teaspoon dried rosemary
½ teaspoon dried thyme
2 skinless, bone-in chicken breasts, or 4 skinless, boneless chicken thighs
5 small new potatoes, quartered
1 (14-ounce) can whole imported Italian tomatoes, roughly chopped
½ teaspoon anchovy paste (optional)
1 cup white wine
1 (14-ounce) can chicken broth
1 cup fresh green beans, trimmed
2 tablespoons tomato paste
1 (14-ounce) can cannellini beans, rinsed and drained
¼ cup chopped fresh flat-leaf parsley
Juice of ½ lemon

Heat the oil in a medium stockpot. Sauté the onion, red pepper, and celery until softened; season with salt and pepper. Add the garlic, oregano, basil, rosemary, and thyme; cook for 1 minute.

Add the chicken, seasoning with salt and pepper. Add the potatoes, tomatoes, anchovy paste (if desired), wine, chicken broth, green beans, and tomato paste. Simmer for 20 minutes.

Add the beans to the stew; cover and simmer another 20 minutes.

Remove the lid, check the seasoning, and continue simmering until broth is slightly thickened (about 10 minutes). Remove from heat, ensuring that the potatoes are tender. Taste and adjust the seasoning if necessary. Swirl in the fresh parsley and the lemon juice.

Serves 8

tipsy TURKEY CHIPOTLE CHILI

Verna, let's talk turkey. Did you know that skinless turkey breast is one of the leanest sources of protein available? And with nutrients such as niacin, selenium, zinc, and vitamins B-6 and B-12, incorporating more turkey breast into your diet can help fight both heart disease and cancer. Ground turkey, turkey breasts, tenderloins, and cutlets are readily available all year long. You don't have to wait for Thanksgiving to get healthy.

Staggeringly yummy. Spiked with chipotle chiles, cinnamon, and beer, this substantial one-pot wonder is a definite diva-do.

1 pound ground turkey
Coarse salt and cracked black pepper, to taste
1 medium onion, chopped
4 garlic cloves, minced
3 tablespoons olive oil
1 (14-ounce) can diced or crushed tomatoes
1 (4-ounce) can diced green chiles, or one large roasted poblano chile, skinned and chopped
1 (12-ounce) bottle of beer
3 tablespoons tomato paste
1, 2, or 3 chopped chipotle chiles in adobo sauce (depending on the amount of heat you prefer)
½ teaspoon ground coriander
1 tablespoon ground cumin
1 tablespoon dried oregano, preferably Mexican
1 tablespoon ground cinnamon
1 teaspoon ancho chile powder
1 (14-ounce) can dark red kidney beans
2 teaspoons chopped fresh cilantro
2 tablespoons fresh lime juice

GARNISHES
Chopped tomato
Shredded cheese
Sour cream
Toasted corn tortillas

Brown the turkey, seasoning with salt and pepper; drain excess fat.

In a stockpot over medium-high heat, sauté the onion and garlic in olive oil.

As the onions become translucent, add the diced tomatoes, green chiles, browned turkey, and beer. Bring to a simmer and add the tomato paste, chipotles, and all the spices except for the fresh cilantro.

Cover and simmer 10 minutes, stirring occasionally.

Rinse the beans, then add and continue to simmer, covered, another 15 minutes over medium-low heat. Taste and adjust the seasoning if necessary.

Uncover and simmer another 5 minutes. Remove from heat and sprinkle with fresh cilantro and lime juice. Garnish if desired.

Serves 6

comforting CHICKEN, TOMATO, and CILANTRO SOUP

Just a sip and slurp away. Comfort your loved ones with the divas' colorful adaptation of good old chicken soup. Tangy tomatoes and fresh lemon juice provide extra vitamin C, while a smattering of fresh cilantro adds an edgy spark of fresh flavor.

1 large sweet onion, chopped
2 celery ribs, chopped
2 carrots, peeled and thinly sliced
4 tablespoons olive oil
Coarse salt and cracked black pepper, to taste
6 cups chicken stock or broth
3 skinless, bone-in chicken breasts
1 (14-ounce) can diced tomatoes
1 cup dry white wine
Juice of 2 lemons
1 bunch fresh cilantro, chopped

In a stockpot, sauté the onions, celery, and carrot in the olive oil until the vegetables are tender and fragrant. Season with salt and pepper.

Add the stock, chicken, tomatoes, and wine; bring to a simmer.

Simmer, uncovered, for 20 minutes, then cover and simmer an additional 15 minutes. Remove chicken breasts and debone. Tear into bite-size pieces and return to the pot. Taste and adjust seasoning, if necessary; add the lemon juice and fresh cilantro.

Serves 8

saucy SAUSAGE POZOLE

Behold a salutary mélange of lean turkey sausage, fresh zucchini, fiber-rich black beans, and old-fashioned white hominy.

½ pound turkey sausage, casings removed
1 medium onion, chopped
Coarse salt and cracked black pepper, to taste
1 (4-ounce) can diced green chiles
4 garlic cloves, minced
1 (14-ounce) can chicken broth
1 (14-ounce) can diced tomatoes
1 (14-ounce) can black beans, rinsed
1 (14-ounce) can pozole, or hominy, drained
½ cup white wine
1 cup diced zucchini (about 1 medium)
1 teaspoon ground cumin
½ teaspoon ground cinnamon
1 teaspoon dried oregano
½ teaspoon chipotle chile powder (optional)
1 tablespoon extra-virgin olive oil
2 tablespoons fresh lime juice
3 tablespoons chopped fresh cilantro
Chopped tomato and avocado (optional)

Sauté the sausage and onion in a medium stockpot over medium heat, lightly seasoning with salt and pepper. Drain excess fat if necessary.

Add the chiles and garlic and continue to sauté for another minute or so.

Add the chicken broth, tomatoes, beans, pozole, and wine; bring to a simmer. Add the zucchini, cumin, cinnamon, oregano, and chile powder; simmer, uncovered, over medium-low heat for 30 minutes.

When the broth has thickened slightly, taste and adjust the seasoning if necessary. Drizzle in the olive oil and lime juice and add the fresh cilantro. Garnish with tomatoes and avocado if desired.

Serves 6

I'M CONFESSIN'

Keep you pantry well stocked—canned chicken broth, diced tomatoes and chiles, beans, and hominy are all you need to deliver a healthful meal in a flash (without ordering a pizza). A dash of lime and a quick flip of fresh herbs brighten flavors. Stock it up!

lotsa MASA MEATBALL STEW with FRESH MINT

Delectable morsels of beef infused with masa harina, *or corn tortilla flour, simmer south-of-the-border style in a light broth. Brimming with fresh veggies and chopped mint, this unparalleled pot of yum will satisfy your next craving for Mexican fare.*

1 pound ground beef or ground turkey
⅓ cup masa harina
Coarse salt and cracked black pepper, to taste
1½ teaspoons ground cumin, divided
1 egg, lightly beaten
4 tablespoons olive oil, divided
3 cups chicken stock, divided
½ medium onion, roughly chopped
4 garlic cloves, minced
1 celery rib, chopped
½ red bell pepper, chopped
1 ear corn, kernels removed, cob reserved

1 (14-ounce) can diced tomatoes
1 (4-ounce) can diced green chiles
1 cup dry white wine
1 teaspoon ground coriander
½ teaspoon ancho chile powder
3 tablespoons fresh mint, chopped
Fresh cilantro (optional)
Fresh mint (optional)
Tortilla chips (optional)
Monterey Jack cheese (optional)

Combine the ground beef, masa, salt, pepper, cumin, and egg in a large bowl. Mix thoroughly, then form into 1½-inch balls.

In a large nonstick skillet, heat 2 tablespoons of the oil and brown the meatballs in batches, being careful not to overcrowd. Once browned, remove and set aside.

Deglaze the pan with 1 cup of the chicken stock, scraping the browned bits from the pan. Simmer for a few minutes, then strain and reserve this liquid.

In a large soup pot, sauté the onions, garlic, celery, and red pepper in the remaining oil. Cook until tender but not browned. Season with salt and pepper.

Add the corn and the corncob, the tomatoes, and the remaining 2 cups stock plus the 1 cup reserved. Stir in the chiles, wine, coriander, and chile powder. Add the browned meatballs to the pot and bring the soup to a simmer. Cover and cook over medium-low heat for 30 minutes.

Remove the lid and allow stock to reduce for 10 minutes. Remove the corn cob and discard. Stir in the fresh mint, check the seasoning, and remove from heat.

Garnish if desired.

Serves 8

PASTA(less) FAGIOLI

I'M CONFESSIN'

To add a gourmet touch, drizzle each serving with extra-virgin olive oil.

There's no need to use your noodle as you throw together our quickie version of this Italian classic.

1 pound lean ground beef
Coarse salt and cracked black pepper, to taste
1 medium onion, chopped
2 celery ribs, chopped
2 tablespoons olive oil
6 garlic cloves, minced
6 tablespoons minced fresh flat-leaf parsley, divided
1 tablespoon dried oregano
1 tablespoon dried basil
1 teaspoon dried thyme
½ teaspoon crushed red pepper (optional)
1 (28-ounce) can crushed tomatoes
3 (14-ounce) cans beef broth
1 cup dry white wine
1 bay leaf
1 (14-ounce) can dark red kidney beans
2 (14-ounce) cans cannellini beans
1 cup prepared spaghetti sauce
2 carrots, grated
Freshly grated Parmesan cheese, to taste, and extra for garnish

Brown the ground beef, seasoning with salt and pepper; drain and set aside. In a large soup pot, sauté the onions and celery in the olive oil. Season with salt and pepper. As the vegetables soften, add the garlic, 3 tablespoons fresh parsley, and the spices. Stir to prevent the garlic from burning.

Add the ground beef to the soup pot, along with the tomatoes, broth, wine, and bay leaf. Bring to a simmer and cook for 15 minutes. Taste for seasoning and adjust if necessary.

Add the beans and spaghetti sauce. Continue simmering for an additional 15 minutes, stirring often. Add the grated carrots; simmer for another 5 minutes.

Stir in the remaining parsley and cheese and remove the soup from heat. Remove the bay leaf. Garnish with additional grated Parmesan if desired.

Serves 10

little LAMB CURRY STEW

Even Mary wouldn't be able to resist this diva-licious twist on classic beef stew. Comforting chunks of buttery potato and earthy bits of tender lamb simmer in a rich curry laced with sherry and Dijon mustard.

1 pound lean ground lamb, or lamb pieces cut for stew
4 tablespoons extra-virgin olive oil, divided
Coarse salt and cracked black pepper, to taste
2 teaspoons dried oregano, divided
1 onion, chopped
2 large carrots, peeled and cut into ½-inch-thick slices
6 garlic cloves, chopped
3 cups chicken or veal stock
3 tablespoons dry sherry
1 cup tomato sauce
2 tablespoons Dijon mustard
1 teaspoon curry powder
½ teaspoon ground cumin
2 cups peeled and diced potatoes
2 tablespoons white vinegar
Fresh flat-leaf parsley, minced (optional)

Sauté the lamb in 2 tablespoons of olive oil; season with salt and pepper and 1 teaspoon of oregano. Drain the fat and set aside.

In a separate soup pot or stockpot, sauté the onions and carrots in the remaining olive oil over medium-high heat; season with salt and pepper. As the vegetables begin to soften, add the garlic and sauté for 1 minute, being careful not to burn.

Add the lamb to the vegetables in the soup pot and stir. Add the stock, sherry, tomato sauce, and mustard. Sprinkle in the curry powder and the cumin, along with the remaining oregano and diced potatoes. Season with salt and pepper. Bring to a simmer, cover, and cook for 20 to 30 minutes or until the potatoes are tender. Drizzle with the vinegar and simmer for 1 minute. Taste and adjust the seasoning if necessary. Garnish with fresh minced parsley if desired.

Serves 8

I'M CONFESSIN'

Curry isn't just one spice; it's a term derived from a South Indian word for "sauce." Spice combinations used to create curries vary dramatically from region to region and depend largely on the traditions and tastes of the chef. Commercial brands of curry powder also vary from mild to hot, hot, hot. Buy curry powder in small amounts as its flavor tends to diminish in just a few months.

harmonious HOT-and-SOUR SOUP

Variations on a theme: toss in fresh shrimp or diced firm tofu instead of pork. Fresh spinach leaves added just before serving make for a souper healthy treat.

Vinegar and white pepper strike a harmonious chord in an Eastern melody of comfort. This balanced mélange of shiitake mushrooms, bamboo shoots, tender pork, and egg swirled in a spicy broth warms body, mind, and spirit.

6 cups chicken stock
10 shiitake mushrooms, thinly sliced
½ pound lean pork loin, cut into small pieces
1 (8-ounce) can bamboo shoots, drained
6 tablespoons rice vinegar
¼ cup frozen peas
¼ cup soy sauce
2 teaspoons sesame oil
1 teaspoon ground white pepper, or more to taste
3 tablespoons cornstarch dissolved in $\frac{1}{3}$ cup water
1 egg, lightly beaten
3 green onions, thinly sliced
Fresh cilantro, chopped, to taste

Bring the chicken stock to a boil in a large saucepan.

Stir in the mushrooms, pork, and bamboo shoots and return to a boil. Reduce heat to low and simmer for 3 minutes, stirring occasionally.

Add the vinegar, peas, soy sauce, sesame oil, and white pepper; simmer for 3 minutes.

Add the cornstarch mixture, stirring until the soup thickens, 2 or 3 minutes.

Remove from heat and add the egg, stirring constantly until the egg resembles long threads. Top with sliced green onions and cilantro.

Serves 8

bayou beauty SHRIMP and SAUSAGE GUMBO

Cue the zydeco music and kick up your heels with a bodacious bowl of bliss, bayou style. Using this saucy Cajun classic sans the okra, lavish your family and friends with a bit of lagniappe, the term used in Southern Louisiana to mean "something extra."

3 tablespoons vegetable oil
1 medium onion, chopped
1 red bell pepper, chopped
2 celery ribs, chopped
Coarse salt and cracked black pepper, to taste
½ teaspoon cayenne pepper
6 garlic cloves, minced
1 pound andouille sausage, split in two and sliced into ½-inch pieces
4 tablespoons all-purpose flour
½ teaspoon dried thyme
4 cups chicken or fish stock
1 cup dry white wine
½ cup crushed tomatoes
1 pound shrimp, cleaned and deveined
3 tablespoons minced fresh flat-leaf parsley
2 green onions, sliced
Hot cooked rice (optional)

In your favorite soup pot, heat the oil; add the onion, red pepper, and celery. Season the vegetables with salt, pepper, and cayenne; sauté until tender. Add the garlic and cook for 1 minute.

Toss in the sausage and cook for 5 minutes. Dust the mixture with flour and dried thyme. Stir until evenly distributed.

Add the stock, wine, and tomatoes; simmer for 20 minutes. Add shrimp.

Cook for 2 minutes or until shrimp are done. Top with parsley and green onions and serve over rice if desired.

Serves 6

• • •

I'M CONFESSIN'

Cajun cuisine was heavily influenced by the French settlers of Louisiana. Mirepoix, the classic soup base, was adapted by Cajun and Creole cultures to include onions, celery, and peppers, which were indigenous to the region. This familiar cooking base in classic bayou fare is referred to as the "holy trinity."

Here's the *dish*—the main attraction, the savory heartthrob of the culinary catwalk. Perfect thighs, posh loins, tender morsels of only the freshest fish bathed in a buttery sauce. It's kind of like finding true love on a plate (a new one every night). Travel to exotic countries without packing a bag, or return to your roots with retro-chic slices of Mom's meat loaf.

Passionate cooks can be so fickle when it comes to dinner—it's hard to pick a favorite. Meat or poultry, fish or vegetarian, you get to play the field. And though it's easy to pick up a rotisserie chicken or toss pasta in boiling water, at least once a week give yourself a little extra time to engage your creativity—you'll reap big benefits from a little kitchen TLC.

NOUS

tipsy gypsy TEQUILA SHRIMP IN AVOCADO-LIME SAUCE

When buying fresh shrimp, look for shiny shells and meat that feels firm against the shell. And ask to smell the shrimp when you're buying it thawed or fresh—it should have a fresh salty smell like the ocean, with no fishy or ammonia odor. We prefer Wild American shrimp from the Atlantic or Gulf of Mexico, with no additives and a sweet taste.

Move those hips with a rose in your lips. A summer-sexy, south-of-the-border concoction has all the right moves yet doesn't play hard to get. Just chop to the beat, sizzle, and splash—culinary instant gratification is yours in just 3 minutes.

3 tablespoons extra-virgin olive oil
1 pound large shrimp, peeled and deveined
3 garlic cloves, minced
½ medium onion, chopped
¼ cup tequila
Salt and freshly ground black pepper, to taste
1 or 2 Hass avocados, peeled and diced
¼ cup fresh lime juice
¼ cup chopped fresh cilantro
Steamed corn tortillas (optional)
Lime wedges (optional)

In a large nonstick skillet over medium-high heat, heat the oil. Sauté the shrimp and garlic for about 2 minutes.

Add the onion and tequila and sauté for another minute or so, seasoning with salt and pepper.

Add the avocado, lime juice, and cilantro and sauté for an additional minute. When the shrimp is pink, transfer to a serving platter. Serve with steamed corn tortillas and lime wedges if desired.

Serves 4

salmon says PANTRY CROQUETTES

No time to play games? Here's a down-to-the-wire dinner solution that covers all the bases. Pantry-friendly canned salmon, though often snubbed for fresh, is fabulous patted into these exquisite little morsels. Dijon, fresh parsley, and a squeeze of lemon add sass to this once-humble fare. Serve with an off-the-shelf lemon mayonnaise, steamed fresh vegetables, and lemon wedges.

1 (15-ounce) can skinless, boneless salmon
2 tablespoons light mayonnaise
2 tablespoons Dijon mustard
1 egg, lightly beaten
1 cup fresh breadcrumbs
1 tablespoon fresh lemon juice
¼ teaspoon hot sauce
½ teaspoon Worcestershire sauce
¼ cup chopped fresh parsley
3 to 4 green onions, thinly sliced, green and white parts
Cracked black pepper, to taste
2 tablespoons extra-virgin olive oil

Combine all ingredients except olive oil in a large bowl and mix thoroughly. Shape into 8 small patties or 6 larger ones.

Heat the olive oil in a nonstick skillet over medium-high heat. Sear the croquettes for 3 to 4 minutes on each side or until nicely browned. Serve immediately.

● ● ●

I'M CONFESSIN'

A healthy diva is a happy diva. Rich in omega-3 fatty acids, wild salmon helps to prevent both heart attacks and strokes. It also helps to lower blood pressure, prevent cancers, relieve depression, and even fight wrinkles! Readily available in cans, it's easy to incorporate this super food into your diet—toss it into salads, or spread it onto bread with chopped egg, pickles, and a dollop of mayonnaise.

I'M CONFESSIN'

Do-ahead divas will love this colorful creation. Make the sauce and pâté up to a day ahead of time, then simply sear the fish just before serving. Ask your fish market for sushi-grade tuna fillets (flash-frozen is fine).

mango tango TUNA with CHICKPEA PÂTÉ

Paradise is not lost. Hip-swaying Mango Tango salsa is a hit with mild-mannered yellowfin tuna and its sidekick, a rich, nutty pâté. These exotic flavors may seem far-fetched, but they're really just a pantry away.

FOR THE SALSA:

1 ripe mango
1 teaspoon hot chile oil (optional)
2 tablespoons chopped fresh cilantro
1 garlic clove, chopped
Juice of ½ lemon
½ teaspoon lemon zest
Coarse salt and cracked black pepper, to taste
1 tablespoon extra-virgin olive oil

FOR THE PÂTÉ:

1 can chickpeas, drained
¼ cup shelled pistachios
2 tablespoons toasted sesame seeds
Juice of 1 lime
Juice of ½ lemon
1 garlic clove, chopped
½ teaspoon curry powder
½ teaspoon ground cumin
½ teaspoon cinnamon
2 tablespoons fresh cilantro, chopped
1 tablespoon olive oil
Coarse salt and cracked black pepper, to taste
2 tablespoons cold water

FOR THE TUNA:

4 fresh sushi-grade yellowfin tuna steaks
Salt and pepper, to taste
2 tablespoons canola oil

To prepare the salsa, combine the first 8 ingredients in a blender; puree until smooth. Set aside.

To prepare the pâté, in a food processor, combine the chickpeas, pistachios, sesame seeds, lime juice, lemon juice, 1 garlic clove, curry powder, cumin, cinnamon, cilantro, olive oil, salt, and pepper. Pulse until blended but still chunky. Add water, 1 tablespoon at a time, if the pâté is too thick.

To prepare the tuna, season the steaks with salt and pepper. Place a skillet with the oil over high heat. Add tuna and cook 1 to 2 minutes on each side, or until desired degree of doneness.

To serve, nestle the pâté next to the fish and top with salsa.

Serves 4

GROUPER therapy

... I'M CONFESSIN'

You can use any mild fish in this recipe—halibut, cod, tilapia, or flounder. And, to keep things interesting, switch the fresh parsley for your favorite fresh herb.

Feel the love. Pearly rafts of tender grouper bathed in a buttery lime sauce, then sprinkled with a toss of pungent capers and fresh green onions. Acceptance is just moments away, as this stress-free entrée is ready to share in just 15 minutes.

4 (6- to 8-ounce) grouper fillets
1 cup all-purpose flour
Coarse salt and cracked black pepper, to taste
1 tablespoon paprika
3 tablespoons light olive oil
½ cup dry white wine
½ cup chicken stock
2 tablespoons capers
4 green onions, sliced
2 tablespoons fresh flat-leaf parsley, minced
4 tablespoons unsalted butter, cut into at least 4 pieces
Juice of 1 lime

Rinse the fillets and pat them dry.

Combine the flour, salt, pepper, and paprika in a shallow bowl for dredging (or use a paper plate, as it makes cleanup easier). Dredge the fillets in the seasoned flour and set aside.

Heat a large nonstick skillet over medium-high heat and add the olive oil. When the oil is hot, add the fish. Sear each side for 3 to 4 minutes or until the flesh is opaque and nicely browned on the outside.

Remove the fillets from the skillet and cover loosely to keep warm.

Wipe out the pan and add the wine and stock. Reduce for 3 to 4 minutes, then add the capers, green onions, and parsley. Simmer another 2 minutes and add the butter, stirring constantly. Remove from heat; taste and adjust the seasoning if necessary. Drizzle in the lime juice. Serve fillets immediately, spooning the warm sauce over top.

Serves 4

upper-crusted HERB-AND-MUSTARD SWORDFISH

Good taste is easy to recognize. A standout dish that oozes just the right amount of savoir faire, this bistro-chic pairing of mustard, wine, and fresh herbs makes a bold statement without turning its back on the simple life.

4 swordfish steaks
Coarse salt and cracked black pepper, to taste
6 tablespoons unsalted butter, melted
3 tablespoons Dijon mustard
2 tablespoons fresh flat-leaf parsley, minced
2 tablespoons fresh tarragon, minced
Splash of dry white wine
Lemon wedges

Preheat oven to 450°.

Rinse the fish and pat dry; sprinkle with salt and pepper and set aside.

In a small bowl, combine the remaining ingredients, stirring well. Spoon about 2 tablespoons of this mixture onto each steak and bake for 15 minutes. Serve immediately.

Serves 4

• • •

I'M CONFESSIN'

Serve this elegant entrée with French green beans sautéed in a bit of good oil, a splash of wine, and a toss of fresh thyme leaves. Just a few minutes in the pan will ensure a crisp-tender texture.

This dish only tastes decadent. Brimming with flavor, style, and nutrition, this is the diet-conscious diva's solution to unrivaled entertaining. Serve with just-wilted fresh spinach topped with a little grated Parmesan.

rapturous roasted CHILEAN SEA BASS with TARRAGON-TOMATO SAUCE

If you think it's butter, but it's not… it's probably Chilean sea bass. Nevertheless, even Mother Nature won't mind being fooled by this deceptive pairing of melt-in-your-mouth sea bass and rapturous red sauce spiked with the licorice bite of fresh tarragon. (Was that a thunderclap I heard?)

1½ pounds Chilean sea bass cut into 4 fillets, skin and bones removed
Coarse salt and cracked black pepper, to taste
Paprika, to taste
3 tablespoons extra-virgin olive oil
½ sweet onion, chopped
2 garlic cloves, minced
½ cup dry white wine
2 cups crushed or diced tomatoes
½ cup chicken stock or broth
20 kalamata olives, pitted
1 teaspoon capers
½ teaspoon dried chervil
½ teaspoon crushed red pepper (optional)
3 tablespoons unsalted butter
3 tablespoons fresh tarragon, chopped

Preheat oven to 400°.

Rinse the fillets and pat dry. Season all over with the salt, pepper, and paprika.

Heat the oil in a large nonstick skillet over medium-high heat. Sear the fillets on each side until golden brown, about 2 minutes. Place in a casserole dish large enough to accommodate the fish and sauce.

In the same skillet, sauté the onion until softened. Stir in the garlic and cook for 1 minute. Pour in the wine, tomatoes, and stock; season with salt and pepper. Add the olives, capers, chervil, and, if desired, crushed red pepper. Bring to a simmer and cook, uncovered, for 10 minutes. The sauce should reduce and thicken as it simmers.

Spoon the sauce around the fillets and bake at 400° for 10 minutes. (Do not pour the sauce over the fish.) If the fillets are thicker than 1½ inches, you may want to roast them a bit longer. The fish is ready when the juices run clear and the meat is opaque.

Carefully remove the fish from the casserole, then swirl the butter and fresh tarragon into the sauce, stirring well.

Divide the sauce onto 4 plates; serve fillets on top. Garnish with additional fresh tarragon if desired, and serve with crusty bread.

Serves 4

spice capades BLACKENED TILAPIA with ONION RELISH

This is a perfect dish
for entertaining. You
can easily prepare the
relish a day or two
ahead. Serve with
thick-sliced, perfectly
ripened tomatoes
drizzled with your
best-quality olive oil,
or smashed potatoes
for something more
robust.

Jump-start the dinner hour with a lip-searing rub of Cajun spices. Paired with mild-mannered tilapia, then heaped with a luscious mound of caramelized onion relish, this unlikely duo brings down the house with each magnificent mouthful.

6 tilapia fillets
1 teaspoon dried basil
2 teaspoons lemon pepper
4 tablespoons Cajun seasoning (or a mixture of paprika, onion powder, garlic powder, cayenne, and thyme)
¼ cup unsalted butter, melted
3 to 4 tablespoons extra-virgin olive oil
Coarse salt, to taste
1 recipe Brown Sugar Bombshell Red Onion Relish, warmed (page 145)

Rinse the fillets and pat dry. Set aside.

Combine the basil, lemon pepper, and Cajun seasoning in a bowl large enough to dredge the fillets in (or a paper plate works fine).

Brush each fillet with melted butter and dredge in seasoning mixture.

Heat a large skillet over medium-high to high heat. Add the oil and cook the fillets for 2 minutes on each side, seasoning lightly with salt. You will probably have to cook the fish in at least 2 batches, so keep the first batch warm as you cook the second.

Top each fillet with equal portions of onion relish. Serve immediately.

Serves 6

mellow yellow SHRIMP in SPICY YOGURT SAUCE

Tender shrimp swept away in a torrent of brilliant yellow curry, these mellifluous flavors speak of India without booking passage.

4 cups water
1 teaspoon turmeric
2 pounds medium to large shrimp, peeled and deveined
3 tablespoons vegetable oil or light olive oil
1 large sweet onion, finely chopped
Coarse salt, to taste
5 garlic cloves, minced
1 teaspoon ground cumin
2 teaspoons ground coriander
½ teaspoon cayenne pepper
¼ cup plain yogurt, preferably whole-milk
2 jalapeño peppers, seeded and minced
¼ cup heavy cream
2 tablespoons fresh cilantro, minced

Bring 4 cups water and the turmeric to a boil; add the shrimp and cook for about 3 minutes. Drain, reserving the cooking liquid; set aside.

Place a large nonstick pan with the oil over medium-high heat. Sauté the onion about 10 minutes until golden brown, then season with salt. Add the garlic and cook for an additional minute. Reduce the heat a bit and add the cumin, coriander, and cayenne pepper, stirring rapidly for about 30 seconds.

Add half of the reserved cooking liquid from the shrimp and raise the heat to high. Boil the mixture for about 10 minutes, stirring often. Add the rest of the liquid and reduce for about another 20 minutes. The sauce should become quite thick. Continue stirring so that the sauce does not stick.

Add the yogurt and jalapeños and cook for another 3 to 4 minutes, stirring constantly until yogurt is thoroughly incorporated. Reduce the heat to low and add the shrimp to the pan. Cook until just heated through (about 2 minutes). Remove the skillet from heat and stir in the cream. Garnish with minced fresh cilantro.

Serves 8

I'M CONFESSIN'

Pick up the pace by purchasing prepared shrimp already peeled and deveined—just give them a rinse, and you're ready to go. We serve these exotic beauties with black rice, or "forbidden rice" (found in most gourmet grocery stores). Studded with fresh green chiles, this intensely yellow curry is a knockout paired with the onyx, nut-scented rice. Also a wonderful choice for entertaining, this entrée improves the longer the flavors develop; just reheat gently, fold in some fresh cilantro, and blow them all away!

perfect THIGHS with lotsa OLIVES

Your quest for perfect thighs is finally over. Nestled in a flattering red sauce, these Mediterranean gams strike a tasteful pose with sweet baby carrots and lotsa olives. Garnish with feta and fresh chopped flat-leaf parsley. Serve with crusty bread, pasta, or risotto.

8 skinless, boneless chicken thighs
Coarse salt and cracked black pepper, to taste
3 or 4 tablespoons flour, for dusting
1 tablespoon or more dried oregano
6 tablespoons extra-virgin olive oil, divided
1 medium onion, chopped
20 baby carrots
1 (14-ounce) can crushed tomatoes
1 cup chicken stock
5 garlic cloves, thinly sliced
1 cup red wine
1 cup pitted kalamata olives
½ cup pitted green olives
2 tablespoons unsalted butter
3 tablespoons fresh flat-leaf parsley, chopped

Season the chicken thighs with salt and pepper, dust lightly with flour, and sprinkle with oregano to taste.

Heat 4 tablespoons of the olive oil in a small stockpot or a large skillet deep enough to hold the chicken thighs and sauce. When the olive oil is hot, sear the thighs 3 to 4 minutes on each side or until nicely browned. Remove from pan; set aside.

Add the chopped onion and carrots to the pan, adding a bit more olive oil if necessary. Season with salt and pepper. Sauté the vegetables until the onion is softened, about 5 minutes. Stir in the crushed tomatoes and chicken stock. Add garlic, wine, and, if desired, more salt. Return chicken to the pan, lower heat, cover, and simmer for 15 minutes, stirring occasionally.

Add the olives and remaining olive oil. Continue to simmer, uncovered, 10 minutes. Remove from heat, stir in butter, and garnish with fresh parsley.

Serves 4

LULU'S RED CURRY thunder THIGHS

Skinny chicks need not apply; only the most Rubenesque thighs will do for this succulent stew of chicken, tomatoes, fresh garlic, mustard, curry, and fresh herbs. Serve with hot basmati rice—or just some good bread. You won't want to waste a drop of the smoky, intoxicating sauce.

8 skinless, boneless chicken thighs
Coarse salt and cracked black pepper, to taste
2 tablespoons extra-virgin olive oil
1 medium onion, chopped
1 celery rib, finely chopped
1 small red pepper, chopped
1 jalapeño pepper, seeded and minced
3 garlic cloves, minced
1 teaspoon curry powder
2 tablespoons stone-ground mustard
1 teaspoon dried oregano
2 tablespoons fresh flat-leaf parsley, chopped
2 tablespoons fresh cilantro, chopped
1 cup white wine
1 cup tomato sauce
1 chicken bouillon cube
Fresh lime juice (optional)
Fresh cilantro (optional)

Season the thighs with salt and pepper. Heat the olive oil in a large skillet over medium-high heat, then sear the thighs on both sides until nicely browned. Remove from pan; set aside.

In the same skillet, sauté the onion, celery, and peppers until softened; add the garlic and sauté for 1 minute. Season the vegetables with salt and pepper. Stir in the curry powder, mustard, and oregano, then the parsley and cilantro. Pour in the wine and tomato sauce; add the chicken bouillon cube, and return the thighs to the pan.

Bring to a boil, then simmer for 10 minutes. Cover and simmer another 5 minutes. Taste and adjust the seasoning if necessary. Sprinkle with fresh lime juice and cilantro.

Serves 4

• • •

I'M CONFESSIN'

Busy week ahead? Make a double batch of this fabulous stew, then freeze half. What could be easier than plucking a delicious meal from your own freezer? (You can catch up with the pizza delivery boy some other time.)

It's easy to slice your own cutlets from whole boneless breasts. With a sharp knife, remove the skin and any fat, then slice the breast into two portions down the middle, creating two breast halves (most packaged breasts come this way). Place the palm of one hand flat on breast half, and slice parallel to the cutting surface into two or three slices, depending on the thickness of the chicken breast. Pound the cutlets between waxed paper using a meat mallet, rolling pin, or, in a pinch, even an empty wine bottle or heavy drinking glass will do.

in a pickle SHIITAKE MEDALLIONS OF CHICKEN

Solving the dinner hour's most provocative question: what new thing might a diva do with boneless chicken breasts? Seemingly artless at first glance, these prepackaged beauties have stumped us all. Well, here's our latest inspiration: a creamy trio of tender, pounded medallions of chicken; shiitake mushrooms; and tart, tiny pickles. Saturday night swank at its finest, but easy enough for busy weeknight fare. Serve over fresh sautéed spinach.

1 pound chicken breast cutlets
1 cup flour for dredging, seasoned with salt and pepper
2 tablespoons olive oil
1 tablespoon unsalted butter
20 fresh shiitake or cremini mushrooms, sliced
¼ cup dry white wine
1 tablespoon Dijon mustard
1½ cups heavy cream
½ cup cornichon pickles, sliced diagonally
2 to 3 tablespoons fresh flat-leaf parsley, chopped
Cracked black pepper, to taste

Place the cutlets between 2 sheets of waxed paper or plastic wrap and pound to ¼-inch thickness.

Dredge chicken pieces in the seasoned flour.

Heat a large nonstick skillet over medium-high heat and add the olive oil. Sear the cutlets, being careful not to overcrowd, for about 3 minutes on each side. Remove the cutlets from the pan and keep warm.

Reduce heat to medium-low and add the butter. Sauté the mushrooms until they begin to release moisture, seasoning lightly with salt and pepper. Add the wine and mustard and simmer for 3 or 4 minutes. Increase the heat to medium, then add the cream and the pickles; simmer an additional 4 minutes, allowing the sauce to thicken and reduce.

Return the cutlets to the pan and spoon the warm sauce over them. Remove the pan from the heat and garnish with fresh minced parsley and a few turns of cracked black pepper.

Serves 4

I'M CONFESSIN'

Although you can't beat the spicy taste of andouille, a heavily smoked sausage made from pork chitterlings and tripe, you can cut calories by substituting chicken or turkey sausage. Good girls also can use half-and-half instead of heavy cream.

bad to the boneLESS CHICKEN BREASTS

Breaking free of her good-girl reputation, skinless, low-fat chicken is hanging with a dangerous crowd. Decadent cream and spicy andouille sausages are heating things up with a swirl of mustard and mushrooms gone wild. But with just one taste, you'll forgive your diet-conscious poultry diva—this road to ruin is worth every calorie.

4 skinless, boneless chicken breasts
4 tablespoons olive oil
1 teaspoon paprika
1 teaspoon onion powder
Coarse salt and cracked black pepper, to taste
4 links andouille sausage, cut into ¼-inch slices (you can substitute chicken or turkey sausage)
2 cups mixed wild mushrooms, or 2 cups cremini mushrooms
1 cup heavy cream
¼ cup Creole mustard
4 green onions, thinly sliced

Preheat oven to 350°.

Rub the chicken breasts with oil, then season with the paprika, onion powder, salt, and pepper. In a casserole dish, bake the breasts at 350° for 20 to 25 minutes or until juices run clear.

Meanwhile, in a large nonstick skillet, sauté the andouille sausage over medium-high heat until nicely browned; discard all of the fat except 1 tablespoon. (If you are using chicken or turkey sausage instead of andouille, you may want to add a bit of oil to the pan while sautéing.)

Add the mushrooms and sauté for 2 minutes, then add the cream, reducing the heat to medium-low. Allow the cream to simmer until it is reduced by one-fourth, about 5 minutes. Add the mustard and reduce until the sauce is thick enough to coat the back of a spoon. Remove from heat.

Spoon sauce over cooked chicken breasts and garnish with sliced green onions.

Serves 4

african queen CHICKEN with TOMATOES AND PEANUTS

No time to travel to Africa? Nothing to wear? Create this African-inspired concoction of chicken, tomatoes, and peanuts, an aromatic stew that conjures the exotic without you having to leave your kitchen.

1 pound chicken tenderloins
Coarse salt and cracked black pepper, to taste
1 large sweet onion, diced
3 tablespoons canola oil
8 garlic cloves, minced
2 (14-ounce) cans diced tomatoes
1 teaspoon ground coriander
3 tablespoons crunchy peanut butter
¼ cup fresh cilantro, minced

Rinse the chicken and pat dry; season with salt and pepper and set aside.

Heat a nonstick skillet large enough to hold all the ingredients. Sauté the onion in the oil, seasoning with salt and pepper, until translucent and fragrant, about 5 minutes. Toss in the chicken pieces and sauté until the chicken is lightly browned.

Add the garlic and cook for 1 minute, being careful not to burn. Pour in the tomatoes and add the coriander and peanut butter; cover and cook for 30 minutes. Taste and adjust the seasoning if necessary. Fold in the fresh cilantro.

Serves 6

. . .

I'M CONFESSIN'

A well-stocked pantry should extend well beyond your cupboards: flash-frozen chicken tenderloins are a versatile staple to keep in your freezer at all times. With no thawing necessary, they are ready to toss into a hot pan right out of the bag. And they're individually frozen, so you can cook for 2 or 20.

I'M CONFESSIN'

The divas adore a gooey mound of goat cheese—but for some, its texture can be problematic. Feta cheese is a wonderful substitute for this recipe if you, or someone you love, does not go for goat.

gobble-licious TURKEY BURGERS with SUN-DRIED TOMATO KETCHUP

Even the hottest buns aren't necessary for these gooey gourmet burgers. With mushrooms, goat cheese, garlic, and an edgy version of homemade ketchup, budget-friendly ground turkey stands alone.

FOR THE KETCHUP:

1 cup oil-packed sun-dried tomatoes, drained
½ cup ketchup
2 tablespoons capers, rinsed
1 teaspoon sugar
2 tablespoons balsamic vinegar
2 tablespoons fresh basil leaves, chopped
Coarse salt and cracked black pepper, to taste

FOR THE BURGERS:

1 pound ground turkey
2 cups sliced mushrooms, sautéed
2 garlic cloves, minced
1 egg, lightly beaten
3 tablespoons fresh flat-leaf parsley, minced
½ cup packaged breadcrumbs or one stale slice of bread, crumbled
6 ounces crumbled goat cheese
Coarse salt and cracked black pepper, to taste
2 tablespoons olive oil

To prepare the ketchup, combine the first 7 ingredients in a blender or food processor; puree and set aside. If too thick, add a bit of water.

To prepare the burgers, in a large bowl combine the turkey, mushrooms, garlic, egg, parsley, breadcrumbs, and goat cheese. Season with salt and pepper; use your hands to mix thoroughly. Form into 6 burgers.

Heat olive oil in a nonstick skillet over medium-high heat. Sear the burgers 5 minutes on each side or until juices run clear. Serve with Sun-Dried Tomato Ketchup.

Serves 6

thai-die-for TURKEY TENDER-LOINS in COCONUT MILK

This is all about a well-stocked pantry, girlfriends—a simmer-licious concoction that only seems exotic. A sashay over to the cupboard, some fresh turkey tenderloins, and you're on your way to an enticing one-pot wonder that will leave them swooning.

2 tablespoons canola oil
1 small onion, chopped
2 tablespoons fresh ginger, minced
2 tablespoons fresh garlic, minced
Coarse salt and cracked black pepper, to taste
1 teaspoon ground cumin
½ teaspoon ground turmeric
1 teaspoon ground coriander
½ teaspoon cayenne pepper
4 turkey tenderloins, cut into bite-size pieces
1 can diced tomatoes
½ cup white wine
1 can chickpeas, rinsed and drained
1 cup canned coconut milk
3 tablespoons fresh cilantro, minced
Juice of 1 one lime

Heat the oil in a large nonstick skillet over medium heat; add onion and sauté until lightly golden. Stir in the fresh ginger and garlic and sauté for 2 minutes, seasoning with salt and pepper.

Add the cumin, turmeric, coriander, and cayenne pepper. Sauté the spices for another 2 minutes (this gives them a wonderful smoky quality).

Add the turkey pieces with some additional oil if needed. Sauté with the onion and herb mixture for 2 to 3 minutes.

Add the tomatoes, wine, and chickpeas. Simmer for 15 to 20 minutes.

Taste and adjust the seasoning if necessary. Add the coconut milk and simmer for 5 minutes, allowing the sauce to thicken slightly. Stir in the cilantro and lime juice. Serve with additional cilantro and lime wedges if desired.

Serves 6

I'M CONFESSIN'

Serve this exotic beauty tossed with pasta and some roasted peanuts—chopsticks make it all the more festive. And if you can't find turkey tenderloins, chicken tenderloins work—fresh or frozen.

chop 'til you drop CHICKEN CURRY

...
I'M CONFESSIN'

This dish is fabulous with the Soothing Cucumber-Yogurt Salad (page 139) and Be Sweet to Me Tomato Chutney (page 143). Fold it all into naan, the East Indian white-flour flatbread found at gourmet or Indian grocery stores.

Time to sharpen that knife, girlfriends. Just a bit of chopping therapy creates this melodious meltdown of intense, smoky flavors that bottled curry powder cannot produce. So pour a glass of wine and resign yourself to the simple pleasures of domesticity (diva-style, of course).

3 tablespoons vegetable oil
1 large sweet onion, finely diced
Coarse salt and cracked black pepper, to taste
2 tablespoons fresh ginger, minced
3 to 4 garlic cloves, minced
2 jalapeño peppers, seeded and chopped
1 teaspoon ground cumin
1 teaspoon ground coriander
½ teaspoon ground turmeric
½ teaspoon cayenne pepper
½ teaspoon chili powder
1 can petite diced tomatoes
3 to 4 boneless chicken breasts, cut into 1½-inch chunks, seasoned with salt
1 tablespoon garam masala
½ cup fresh cilantro, chopped

In a large skillet, heat the oil over medium heat, and sauté the onion until golden, about 10 minutes. Season with salt and pepper.

Add the ginger, garlic, and jalapeños and stir-fry for about 2 minutes, seasoning again with another pinch of salt. Add all the dry spices and stir-fry until slightly puffed, about 2 minutes.

Pour in the diced tomatoes and stir to combine. Add the chicken and cook for 20 minutes, stirring often. When the chicken is cooked through, add the garam masala. Reduce heat to low for about 2 minutes. Remove from heat and sprinkle with fresh cilantro.

Serves 4 to 6

simmerin' summer CHICKEN AND VEGGIES

This healthy chick positively sizzles: fresh summer produce mingled with wine, spices, and tender, juicy thighs. Serve with pasta or some good bread—the dilly sauce is wonderful!

3 tablespoons extra-virgin olive oil
8 skinless, boneless chicken thighs
Coarse salt and cracked black pepper, to taste
1 teaspoon dried oregano
1 medium onion, chopped
2 carrots, peeled and chopped
1 red bell pepper, chopped
4 garlic cloves, thinly sliced
2 tablespoons fresh basil, chopped
2 tablespoons fresh flat-leaf parsley, chopped
1 teaspoon dried dill
6 plum tomatoes, chopped, or 1 (14-ounce) can tomatoes, drained
½ cup dry white wine
2 medium zucchini, sliced into ¼-inch rounds
1 teaspoon red wine vinegar
Freshly grated Parmesan cheese, to taste

Heat the oil in a large sauté pan deep enough to contain the chicken, veggies, and sauce. Brown the chicken pieces, seasoning with salt, pepper, and oregano. Remove the chicken and set aside.

Add the onion, carrots, pepper, garlic, basil, parsley, and dill to the same pan. Sauté until vegetables are tender and fragrant. Pour in the tomatoes and wine and simmer for 5 minutes.

Return the chicken to the pan; cover and simmer for 20 minutes. Taste and adjust seasoning if necessary. Add the zucchini and simmer until tender, about 6 minutes. Sprinkle with the vinegar. Serve with freshly grated Parmesan.

Serves 4 to 6

If you're entertaining, use fresh corn. Otherwise, just grab a bag of frozen and go with that. One of the best features of this yummy concoction is that it cooks up in one big pan, so cleaning up (the very worst aspect of cooking for any diva) is a cinch. Nonstick pans are helpful, too. Delicious with a simple green salad or sliced avocados.

chi-chi-poo-poo CHIPOTLE CHICKEN AND RICE

This is inspired comfort food—a cozy favorite accessorized with a few novel ingredients. Fresh corn, crisp bacon, smoky chipotle sauce, and a dollop of Dijon make over Granny's humble offerings in super style. One pot, numerous accolades—how could you go wrong?

8 ounces bacon, chopped
4 skinless, bone-in chicken breasts (the bones help to flavor the sauce)
Coarse salt and cracked black pepper, to taste
1 tablespoon dried oregano
3 tablespoons extra-virgin olive oil
½ large sweet onion, chopped
2 celery ribs, chopped
2 carrots, peeled and grated (you can slice these if preferred)
1 (14.5-ounce) can diced tomatoes
1 teaspoon ground cumin
1 bay leaf
1 cup corn (2 ears fresh, shaved from cob, or 1 cup frozen)
2 tablespoons Dijon mustard
½ cup dry white wine
1 chipotle pepper with 1 tablespoon of adobo sauce
1 cup white basmati rice
2 cups chicken stock
¼ cup fresh cilantro, minced
¼ cup fresh flat-leaf parsley, minced
4 green onions, chopped

In a large nonstick skillet, cook the bacon until crisp; drain on paper towels, wiping the grease from the pan (you may want to leave just a little behind).

Season the chicken breasts with salt and pepper to taste, rubbing with the oregano on both sides. Heat the olive oil over medium-high heat; when hot, add the chicken breasts and sear for about 4 minutes on each side (you want to get some good color on them and a bit of a crisp crust to hold in the moisture of the meat as it simmers). When nicely browned, remove the chicken and set aside.

In the same pan, sauté the onions, celery, and carrots, seasoning with salt and pepper.

When the vegetables are softened and fragrant, add the tomatoes, cumin, bay leaf, mustard, wine, and chipotle pepper with adobo sauce. Stir in the corn and reduce heat to medium; cover and simmer for about 10 minutes.

Add the chicken to the sauce and cook for another 20 minutes or until the meat is cooked through. Remove the chicken from the pan again and keep warm.

Add the rice and chicken stock to the sauce and bring to a gentle simmer; cover and cook until the rice is tender, about 20 minutes. Remove bay leaf. Stir in the crumbled bacon.

Serve in a large bowl, with the chicken on top. Garnish with a mixture of fresh cilantro, parsley, and chopped green onions.

I'M CONFESSIN'

If you've ever made old-fashioned gravy from the meat drippings coating the bottom of a roasting pan, you've already mastered deglazing, another one of those anxiety-producing cooking terms. Simply remove excess fat from the pan, then deglaze by stirring the caramelized brown bits from the bottom of the pan with wine, broth, or water . . . and voilà! You've got sauce. (And it makes cleanup a whole lot easier, too.)

rich chick ROASTED CHICKEN with WINE, PARSLEY, and GARLIC

You could travel to Paris to sample this bistro classic. Or, if you're just too hungry to make it across the Atlantic, you can fashion this French beauty in no time flat. In this case, the name says it all: a golden roasted bird with crispy skin and a blissful sauce to drizzle over all. Oh, and it comes together in just one pot, leaving you with the simple task of asking the butler to make a salad.

6 or so pieces of chicken, skin on and bone in
Coarse salt and cracked black pepper, to taste
1 tablespoon herbes de Provence
2 tablespoons olive oil
6 tablespoons unsalted butter, divided
1 cup dry white wine
4 garlic cloves, thinly sliced
¼ cup parsley, chopped

Rinse the chicken and pat dry; season with salt and pepper, and rub with the herbes de Provence.

In a Dutch oven big enough to hold all the chicken pieces, heat the olive oil and 3 tablespoons butter over medium-high to high heat. When the butter is sizzling, place the chicken pieces in the pot, skin side down, and sear for 4 minutes. Turn the chicken and reduce the heat to medium; cover and cook for 40 minutes, turning occasionally. When the chicken is cooked through, remove to a platter and keep warm.

Pour all the fat from pan except for 1 tablespoon, and return to the heat; deglaze the pan with the wine, scraping all the flavorful browned bits from the bottom. Allow the wine to simmer and reduce by about half, about 4 or 5 minutes.

Stir in the garlic and parsley and cook for 4 minutes. Remove the pan from the heat and whisk the butter into the sauce. Pour the sauce over the chicken and serve.

deceptively delicious MEAT LOAF with BALSAMIC GLAZE

The shoe-shopping addict's recipe for subterfuge: leave the bags in the trunk, then smuggle them in while your meat-and-potatoes sweetie devours a plate of retro-chic redemption. Complete this maneuver with a mound of garlic mashed potatoes.

FOR THE MEAT LOAF

1 pound ground sirloin or ground turkey
½ cup ketchup
½ cup fresh breadcrumbs
¼ cup fresh flat-leaf parsley, chopped
3 garlic cloves, minced
1 small onion, minced
1 egg
2 teaspoons dried tarragon
1 teaspoon dried basil
1 egg
⅓ cup grated Parmesan, kasseri, or Swiss cheese
1 teaspoon coarse salt
Cracked black pepper, to taste

FOR THE GLAZE:

½ cup ketchup
2 tablespoons balsamic vinegar
2 tablespoons honey
1 teaspoon hot sauce

Preheat oven to 375°.

To prepare the meat loaf, in a large bowl, combine the first 13 ingredients . Mix with your hands (or, if squeamish, this is something little kids love to do).

Shape mixture into a smooth oval shape in an ovenproof baking dish.

To prepare the glaze, mix together the remaining ingredients and brush over the meat loaf. Bake at 375° for 45 minutes. Allow the loaf to rest for at least 5 minutes before slicing.

Serves 4

I'M CONFESSIN'

Between whole-grain slices of bread with slices of ripe tomato, fresh avocado, and a dollop of mayonnaise, cold meat loaf is the classic comfort food. (You can always start your diet next Monday).

This recipe is super quick, yet tastes as if you slaved for hours. Of course, any sort of smashed potatoes would be a fabulous choice for a side, but we love this dish with Put Me on a Pedestal Purple Cabbage with Crumbled Goat Cheese and Toasted Walnuts (page 67). The pungent bite of the cheese contrasts nicely with the tart glaze, while the slightly crunchy cabbage is fabulous with the tender, savory pork.

such a pleaser PORK TENDERLOIN with BALSAMIC GLAZE

Learning to say "no" is a wise thing indeed, but you'll want to say "yes" to entertaining with this easy, elegant entrée that is virtually foolproof.

2 (¾-pound) pork tenderloins
Coarse salt and cracked black pepper, to taste
1 teaspoon dried rosemary
2 tablespoons extra-virgin olive oil
2 cups balsamic vinegar
3 tablespoons sugar, or honey if preferred

Preheat oven to 375°.

Season the tenderloins with salt, pepper, and rosemary.

In a large nonstick pan, heat the oil over medium-high heat; sear the pork on all sides until nicely browned. Transfer to a roasting pan and bake at 375° until meat thermometer registers 160°, about 20 minutes.

While the tenderloins roast, make the glaze. In a small saucepan, combine the vinegar and sugar. Bring to a boil and reduce by half, stirring occasionally. This should take about 30 minutes. (The vinegar smell is quite pungent, so if you have an infant or small children, turn on the exhaust fan and keep them out of the kitchen.)

Allow the tenderloin to rest 10 minutes before slicing into ¼-inch-thick rounds. Drizzle with the balsamic glaze.

Serves 6

irresistible HERB-CRUSTED PORK LOIN ROAST

● ● ●

I'M CONFESSIN'

Even your toughest critics will applaud this easy, economical crowd-pleaser. Perfect for the holidays or any special occasion, this savory herb-licious roast is great with Booty-licious Black Beans (page 63) and Lovely Latin Herb-and-Veggie Relish (page 144)

4 garlic cloves, chopped
1 teaspoon coarse salt
Cracked black pepper, to taste
½ teaspoon dried rosemary
½ teaspoon ground cumin
½ teaspoon dried oregano
1 tablespoon extra-virgin olive oil
1 (2-pound) boneless pork loin roast
Juice of 2 limes
2 tablespoons orange juice
2 tablespoons dry white wine

Preheat oven to 400°.

Using a mortar and pestle, make a paste with the garlic, salt, pepper, rosemary, cumin, oregano, and olive oil.

Cut small slits all over the roast and rub with the garlic paste, forcing the mixture into the slits.

Bake at 400° for 20 minutes, turning once to ensure even browning.

In a small bowl, combine the lime juice, orange juice, and wine.

Reduce the heat to 325° and pour the juice mixture over the roast. Cook until a meat thermometer register 160°, about 40 minutes, basting with pan juices every 10 to 15 minutes. Allow to rest at least 10 minutes before serving.

Serves 6

If you don't have a mortar and pestle, finely mince the garlic and rosemary. Add the pepper, cumin, and oregano. Mix in the salt and olive oil to form a paste-like consistency. (Then put "mortar and pestle" on your birthday wish list.)

FETA-stuffed LAMB BURGERS

... I'M CONFESSIN'

If you can't find ground lamb in your grocer's meat department, ask the butcher to grind a small lamb roast for you. Be sure it is lean. If you're not a fan of lamb, substitute ground turkey. Soothing Cucumber-Yogurt Salad (page 139) and Born to Chop Chickpea Salad (page 37) make this dish a meal.

You're the Grecian goddess of the backyard barbecue with these decadent, earthy morsels of rosemary-spiked lamb stuffed with melted feta cheese to nestle inside an oversize bun.

1 pound lean ground lamb
Coarse salt and cracked black pepper, to taste
1 teaspoon dried rosemary, or more, to taste
6 ounces crumbled feta cheese

Season the meat with the salt, pepper, and rosemary. Mix with your hands.

Divide the lamb into 8 equal portions, forming each into a thin patty.

Divide the feta into 4 equal portions.

Place one portion of cheese in the center of a lamb patty, and top with another patty, pressing the edges together so that the cheese is contained in the burger. Repeat this process to form 4 stuffed patties.

Grill or pan-sear the burgers 4 minutes on each side or until desired degree of doneness.

Serves 4

beloved BEEF STEW with HERBES de PROVENCE

The homebody's recipe for romance: a cozy fire, soft blanket, bottle of good red wine, one bowl, two spoons.

1 cup all-purpose flour
Coarse salt and cracked black pepper, to taste
1 teaspoon paprika
1 teaspoon ground cumin
2 pounds beef stew meat, cut into chunks
4 tablespoons extra-virgin olive oil
1 large onion, chopped
5 carrots, peeled and cut into 1-inch rounds
3 large baking potatoes, peeled and chopped
2 cups white wine
4 cups beef stock
3 tablespoons herbes de Provence
3 tablespoons Dijon mustard
2 bay leaves
3 tablespoons fresh parsley, minced
3 tablespoons unsalted butter
2 tablespoons prepared demi-glace (optional, available at gourmet grocery stores)

Combine the flour, salt, pepper, paprika, and cumin. Dredge the beef in the seasoned flour; shake off excess.

Over medium-high heat, add the oil to a large skillet or Dutch oven large enough to hold all the ingredients. Sear the meat until nicely browned. (You may need to do this in batches, as the beef will merely steam if overcrowded.)

When the meat is browned, remove it from the pan and set aside.

In the same pan, add the onion and sauté until softened. Add the carrots, potatoes, wine, stock, herbes de Provence, mustard, and bay leaves. Bring to a simmer and cook, covered, 1½ hours, stirring occasionally. Remove the lid and simmer an additional 45 minutes or until the sauce is thickened. Remove the bay leaves. Taste and adjust the seasoning if necessary. Just before serving, add the parsley, butter, and, if desired, demi-glace, stirring well.

Serves 10

- - -

I'M CONFESSIN'

A big pot of savory stew is a wonderful way to feed a crowd. Why not plan a soup night party with neighbors, family, and friends? Make two soups the day before you're entertaining, then add a simple green salad and some crusty bread to accompany. Keep things simple with disposable bowls, napkins, and flatware. Forget a formal table and let your guests congregate wherever they choose—that's part of the fun.

luscious LAMB MEATBALLS in TOMATO-CINNAMON SAUCE

I'M CONFESSIN'

Instead of spaghetti, reveal this fabulous meatball makeover by serving with orzo, a small rice-like pasta featured in many Greek dishes.

Creativity on the lam? Make over an old favorite, spaghetti and meatballs, with ground lamb, cinnamon, and a toss of fresh mint.

FOR THE MEATBALLS:

1 pound ground lamb
1 teaspoon coarse salt
Cracked black pepper, to taste
1 egg, slightly beaten
3 tablespoons tomato paste
½ to ¾ cup fresh breadcrumbs
1 tablespoon dried oregano
1 teaspoon ground cinnamon
1 tablespoon fresh rosemary, minced
2 tablespoons olive oil

FOR THE SAUCE:

2 tablespoons olive oil
1 medium onion, chopped
4 garlic cloves, minced
½ cup dry red wine
2 (15-ounce) cans whole Italian tomatoes
Coarse salt and cracked black pepper, to taste
1 teaspoon ground cinnamon
1 teaspoon dried oregano
1 tablespoon fresh rosemary, minced
½ cup fresh parsley, minced
Fresh mint, chopped (optional)

To prepare the meatballs, combine the first 10 ingredients. Shape into 1- to 2-inch balls. In a large nonstick pan over medium-high heat, brown the meatballs in batches, forming a nice crust but not cooking all the way through. Remove them from the pan and set aside.

To prepare the sauce, in a stockpot heat 2 tablespoons of olive oil. Sauté the onion until translucent and fragrant, about 5 minutes. Add the garlic and cook for 1 minute, being careful not to burn.

Pour in the wine and tomatoes, breaking up the tomatoes with a wooden spoon. Season with salt, pepper, cinnamon, oregano, and rosemary. Bring to a simmer and cook for about 20 minutes, uncovered. The sauce should reduce a bit, becoming thick and bubbly.

Add the meatballs; cover and simmer for 30 minutes. If the sauce is too thin, remove the meatballs and simmer, uncovered, until slightly reduced. Stir in the fresh parsley. Garnish with chopped fresh mint if desired.

Serves 8

rockin' rolled STUFFED FLANK STEAK with SAUSAGE, MUSHROOMS, and TARRAGON

A star is born. Flaunt this flashy flank, dressed to the nines in a standout sausage stuffing that defies all limits of self-control.

FOR THE STUFFING:

2 tablespoons extra-virgin olive oil
1 large onion, finely diced
Coarse salt and cracked black pepper, to taste
½ pound sweet Italian sausage (pork or turkey), casings removed, crumbled
2 cups favorite mushrooms, sliced
2 garlic cloves, minced
½ cup dry white wine
Pinch of dried tarragon
Pinch of dried chervil
Pinch of lemon pepper
Pinch of orange rind
Pinch of fennel seed
2 tablespoons unsalted butter
½ cup fresh breadcrumbs
4 tablespoons fresh tarragon, chopped

FOR THE STEAK:

1 (2-pound) flank steak, butterflied (you can ask your butcher to do this for you)
Coarse salt and cracked black pepper, to taste
1 teaspoon herbes de Provence
Kitchen twine
1 tablespoon olive oil

Preheat the oven to 400°.

To prepare the stuffing, in a large nonstick skillet heat 2 tablespoons oil until shimmering. Sauté the onion over medium heat until caramelized, about 15 minutes. Season with salt and pepper. Add the sausage and cook for 5 minutes, breaking apart with a wooden spoon. Add the mushrooms, garlic, wine, and spices; cook for 15 minutes. Melt the butter in the mixture, then fold in the breadcrumbs. Stir in tarragon and remove from heat. Set aside.

To prepare the steak, let it sit at room temperaturewhile you make the stuffing. Generously season the steak with salt, pepper, and herbes de Provence.

Lay the steak flat on a work surface and cover with the stuffing mixture. Carefully roll the meat and tie with twine.

In a large skillet, brown the roast in 1 tablespoon olive oil over medium-high heat for a few minutes. Transfer to a roasting pan and bake at 400° for 1 ½ hours. Allow the steak to sit for 10 minutes before slicing.

Serves 6

holy mole PORK

Cocoa-loco chunks of savory pork simmer in a south-of-the-border sauce that only tastes complex. Throw together this cheater's version of authentic Mexican mole in just 45 minutes.

2 pounds pork loin, cut into bite-size chunks
Coarse salt and cracked black pepper, to taste
3 tablespoons olive oil
1 large Spanish onion, finely diced
1 teaspoon ground cumin
1 tablespoon dried oregano
1 teaspoon paprika
½ teaspoon cinnamon
5 garlic cloves, minced
2 teaspoons unsweetened cocoa
1 (14-ounce) can tomato sauce
1 (6-ounce) can green chiles
Juice of 1 lime
4 tablespoons fresh cilantro, minced

Season the pork with salt and pepper. Heat the oil in a skillet large enough to hold both the meat and the sauce. Sear the meat in 2 batches, being careful not to overcrowd. Remove the browned pork from the pan and set aside.

Add the diced onion to the pan with a bit of extra oil if needed. Season with cumin, oregano, paprika, cinnamon, salt, and pepper. Allow the onion to wilt, stirring often. Add the garlic and cook for 1 minute. Add the cocoa, tomato sauce, and chiles, stirring well.

Add the meat back to the skillet; cover and simmer for 45 minutes, stirring often. Taste and adjust the seasoning if necessary. Just before serving, add the lime juice and cilantro.

Serves 8

very veggie TACOS with ROASTED TOMATILLO SAUCE

Stuff warm corn tortillas with crisp-tender summer veggies and just-melted goat cheese, then crown with a verdant sauce of sweet roasted tomatillos, herbs, and splash of lime juice. This recipe is the zenith of vegetarian tacos.

2 tablespoons extra-virgin olive oil
2 zucchini, sliced diagonally
2 yellow summer squash, sliced diagonally
1 sweet red pepper, cored and chopped
1 medium onion, sliced vertically
2 ears corn, kernels removed
½ teaspoon ground cumin
Coarse salt and cracked black pepper, to taste
2 garlic cloves, sliced
1 tablespoon fresh lime juice

8 soft corn tortillas
8 ounces crumbled goat cheese
1 recipe Roasted Tomatillo Sauce (page 141)
Chopped fresh cilantro (optional)

Heat the oil in a large nonstick skillet over high heat. Add the zucchini, yellow squash, red pepper, onion, and corn to the pan, seasoning with cumin, salt, and pepper. Sear until crisp-tender, adding the garlic during the last minute of cooking time. Drizzle with lime juice; set aside and keep warm.

Wrap the tortillas in plastic wrap; heat in microwave for 40 seconds on full power.

Divide the cheese equally among the tortillas; top with vegetable mixture, then the warmed sauce. Garnish with chopped fresh cilantro if desired, and serve immediately.

Serves 4

● ● ●
I'M CONFESSIN'

Serve this healthful summer treat with Spanish rice, black beans, and hot sauce. Use leftover sauce to top cheese and olive omelets for brunch the next day, or serve chilled with toasted pita chips.

summer love SIMPLE PASTA

I'M CONFESSIN'

If you're the cook (even on vacation), this is perfect fare— you can make it in less than 30 minutes, then serve at room (or beach) temperature.

A day at the beach, make this lazy-girl epicurean combo in sandy flip-flops and damp sarong. Listen to Dean Martin, sip wine. Let the moon hit your eye like a big pizza pie.

4 tablespoons extra-virgin olive oil, divided
2 cups grape tomatoes, halved
Coarse salt and cracked black pepper, to taste
4 garlic cloves, minced
½ cup white wine
½ cup chicken stock
½ cup pitted kalamata olives, or more, to taste
1 tablespoon capers
2 tablespoons torn fresh basil
3 tablespoons fresh flat-leaf parsley, minced
Juice of 1 lemon
2 tablespoons unsalted butter
1 pound angel-hair pasta or linguine, cooked per package directions
Fresh basil (optional)
Fresh flat-leaf parsley (optional)

Heat 2 tablespoons of the olive oil in a large nonstick skillet over medium-high heat. Add tomatoes, seasoning with salt and pepper. Sauté for a minute or so, then add the garlic, being careful not to burn.

Add the wine and the stock and simmer for 5 minutes. Add the olives and capers and check for seasoning, adjusting if necessary. Simmer another few minutes or until the sauce is slightly thickened. Stir in the basil, parsley, lemon, and butter. Remove from heat.

Cook the pasta according to package directions; drain and add to the sauce. Toss to evenly distribute the olives and tomatoes. Drizzle with 2 tablespoons of olive oil and garnish with black pepper, fresh basil, and parsley if desired.

Serve hot or at room temperature.

Serves 6

PENNE for your thoughts PASTA with ROASTED VEGGIES and GOAT CHEESE

Thirty for dinner? No sweat. We've got it covered with an ooey-gooey medley of tender pasta, roasted veggies and goat cheese. Toss together a big green salad, and you're done. (Double or triple this recipe to feed a crowd.)

1 red bell pepper, seeded and cut into 1-inch squares
1 medium eggplant, cubed
2 yellow squash, cubed
2 zucchini, cubed
1 small onion, coarsely chopped
8 garlic cloves, peeled
Coarse salt and cracked black pepper, to taste
1 tablespoon dried oregano
1 tablespoon dried basil
6 tablespoons extra-virgin olive oil, divided
½ cup dry white wine
1 pound penne pasta, prepared according to package directions
2 cups crumbled goat cheese
2 tablespoons fresh lemon juice
¼ cup pine nuts, toasted (optional)
12 fresh basil leaves, roughly torn (optional)

Preheat the oven to 400°.

In a roasting pan, toss together the bell pepper, eggplant, yellow squash, zucchini, onion, and whole garlic cloves. Season with salt and pepper to taste. Mix in the oregano and basil. Add 4 tablespoons of olive oil, then wine, and stir. Bake at 400° until tender, about 30 minutes, stirring once or twice.

Toss the cooked pasta with the remaining 2 tablespoons of olive oil. Add the goat cheese, stirring well. Stir in the lemon juice.

Remove roasted veggies from the oven and toss with the pasta. Taste and adjust the seasoning if necessary.

Garnish with toasted pine nuts and fresh torn basil if desired.

Serves 8

• • •

I'M CONFESSIN'

Carb angst? Toss the veggies with the goat cheese and forget the pasta. Try a drizzle of balsamic glaze over all—you won't miss the noodles at all.

These are the divas' culinary odds and ends: sauces, salad dressings, relishes, and raitas. Just as the perfect pair of new shoes completes an outfit, these little touches can make a menu sparkle. Diva cuisine is in the details.

RAS

mama lu's MUSTARD VINAIGRETTE

A natural beauty is always in vogue. Dress greens to impress with this classic homemade vinaigrette—easy and all natural, it's much healthier than those bottle-blond varieties.

2 tablespoons Dijon mustard
½ teaspoon kosher salt
Cracked black pepper, to taste
2 tablespoons red wine vinegar
1 tablespoon fresh lemon juice
1 tablespoon honey
1 teaspoon chopped fresh herbs, such as tarragon, chervil, marjoram, and basil
1 large garlic clove, minced
⅓ cup extra-virgin olive oil

Combine all ingredients except olive oil in a small bowl, and stir well with a whisk. Slowly add the olive oil, whisking until thoroughly mixed.

Serves 8

call me sophia ITALIAN TOMATO VINAIGRETTE

Call me Sophia; just don't call me later for amore. Toss with potatoes and Cheddar cheese, or serve with warm bread and a platter of Italian meats and cheeses.

1 teaspoon garlic powder
1 teaspoon dried oregano
½ teaspoon dried basil
Coarse salt and cracked black pepper, to taste
1 tablespoon tomato paste
3 tablespoons red wine vinegar
1 tablespoon fresh lemon juice
¼ cup extra-virgin olive oil

Combine all ingredients except olive oil in a small bowl, and stir well with a whisk. Slowly add the olive oil, whisking until thoroughly mixed.

Serves 8

DIPPETY new

Tart, salty, and sweet flavors (and just a little fire) come together to inspire your desire to dip. This Vietnamese dipping sauce will keep for several days in the fridge. It is fabulous for dunking shrimp, chicken, steak, whatever—and delicious in Asian-inspired noodle soup.

2 garlic cloves, minced
1 hot red chile, seeded and finely sliced
1 (½-inch) piece fresh ginger, peeled and finely minced
3 tablespoons fish sauce
Juice of 1 lime
5 tablespoons water
2 tablespoons sugar

Combine all ingredients in a small bowl, and stir well with a whisk

Makes ½ cup.

soothing CUCUMBER-YOGURT SALAD

At last, you're the queen of cool. Serve this concoction with lamb or curries, or fold it into wraps.

4 Kirby cucumbers, peeled and finely chopped, or grated if desired
Coarse salt and cracked black pepper, to taste
1 teaspoon fresh lemon juice
2 tablespoons fresh mint leaves, finely chopped
½ small sweet onion, minced
1 ½ cups plain yogurt

Place the cucumbers in a colander; season with salt and pepper and allow to drain for 20 minutes. Squeeze out the excess moisture.

Combine cucumbers and remaining ingredients in a medium bowl, and chill for 30 minutes before serving.

Serves 4 as a salad, 8 as a condiment

... glow for GUACAMOLE

Mom's appliances never did justice to avocados. Glorious, jade-green chunks smashed to smithereens with a twist of lemon, a toss of minced garlic, and a drop or two of heat—a shining example of "Less is more." Serve with toasted pita wedges, atop salads, or, my favorite, piled into a meat loaf sandwich.

4 ripe Hass avocados, halved and pitted
1 garlic clove, finely minced
Juice of ½ lemon
Coarse salt and cracked black pepper, to taste
½ teaspoon hot sauce

Using a spoon, scoop out the meat of the avocado and empty into a bowl. Mash the avocado with the remaining ingredients. Taste and adjust the seasoning if necessary.

roasted TOMATILLO SAUCE

Like a salsa—but with a sweet, buttery edge.

1 pound fresh tomatillos, husked and cut into quarters
½ large sweet onion, cut into quarters
3 cloves garlic, chopped
2 tablespoons olive oil
Coarse salt and cracked black pepper to taste
½ teaspoon ground cumin seed
1 (14-ounce) can chicken stock
½ cup white wine
3 corn tortillas, cut into strips
1 tablespoon olive oil
1 fresh poblano pepper
1 tablespoon fresh lemon juice
1 tablespoon best quality extra-virgin olive oil

Preheat oven to 400 degrees.

Combine the tomatillos, onion, and garlic in an oven-safe casserole. Drizzle with olive oil and season with salt, pepper, and cumin. Roast for 25–30 minutes, or until the vegetables are tender and fragrant. Remove from the oven; turn on broiler.

While vegetables roast, combine the chicken stock and wine in a small stock pot. Bring to a boil and reduce by half.

In a nonstick pan over medium-high heat, add the olive oil and sauté the tortilla strips, seasoning with salt and pepper. Combine with the reduced stock. Remove from stovetop to cool.

Broil the poblano pepper on a cookie sheet until skin is completely blackened—about 10 minutes. Remove the pepper from the broiler and put in a small paper bag to cool. Once the pepper has cooled, slip off the skins and discard.

Combine the roasted vegetables, the stock mixture, and the roasted pepper in a blender; puree until smooth. Pour mixture back into the stock pot and taste, correcting seasoning if necessary. Simmer over low heat for 10 minutes.

Remove from heat and add lemon juice and extra-virgin olive oil, stir well.

Makes 3 cups

I'M CONFESSIN'

Roasting the tomatillos adds depth and brings out a wonderful sweetness. This is a delicious sauce for veggies, chicken, fish, or pork tenderloin—or you could chill it in your fridge and serve with tortilla chips.

be sweet to me TOMATO CHUTNEY

Curry favor with simmered tomatoes, ginger, and garlic—then add some sugar and spice and everything nice. Fold sweetly into wraps, or serve alongside Indian dishes.

1 small onion, chopped
2 tablespoons canola oil or light olive oil
2 tablespoons minced fresh ginger
2 tablespoons minced fresh garlic
½ teaspoon ground cardamom
½ teaspoon ground cumin
½ teaspoon ground coriander
½ teaspoon turmeric
½ teaspoon cayenne pepper
1 (14-ounce) can diced tomatoes, or 2 cups chopped fresh tomatoes
1 tablespoon sugar
Juice of 1 lime (optional)

Sauté the onions in the oil in a large skillet over medium-low heat until golden brown, or caramelized (this takes about 15 to 20 minutes).

Add the ginger, garlic, cardamom, cumin, coriander, turmeric, and cayenne pepper, stirring so that the garlic does not burn. Cook for 2 minutes.

Add the tomatoes and sugar, increasing the heat to medium high. Simmer for 20 minutes, stirring often, until sauce is thickened and bubbly. Sprinkle with lime juice if desired.

Serves 8

• • • I'M CONFESSIN'

Canned tomatoes do just fine here. Also, you can find jarred ginger paste in your produce section— using it is much easier than mincing, and it frees you up to put on a little lipstick before your man gets home. Also, this is great for all you do-ahead divas; it can be stored in the fridge for several days.

Girlfriends, I was born to chop, but must also confess that I suffer from food processor paranoia. Tortured by technology, I have honed my knife skills to the point of never needing to drag the thing out, its pieces and parts never seeming to cooperate. However, if you are at peace with modern gadgetry and prefer to pulse, this relish will come together in a flash.

lovely latin HERB-AND-VEGGIE RELISH

With lively flavor, this exotic beauty is a natural with savory roast pork or grilled fish. It may be chilled in the fridge for up to three days.

1 small onion, finely minced
1 carrot, finely minced
3 garlic cloves, minced
½ green pepper, finely minced
½ red pepper, finely minced
1 bunch fresh flat-leaf parsley, minced
¼ cup minced fresh cilantro
1 teaspoon dried oregano
1 teaspoon ground cumin
1 ripe tomato, finely diced and drained
of excess juices
2 tablespoons white wine vinegar
3 tablespoons extra-virgin olive oil
Coarse salt and cracked black pepper, to taste

Combine all ingredients except the salt and black pepper in a nonreactive bowl; toss well.

Allow flavors to marry for at least 30 minutes before serving. Add salt and pepper to taste.

Serves 12

brown sugar bombshell,
RED ONION RELISH

*This is ooey-gooey food at its finest. Really, you could serve this with anything—
even cardboard—but do try it with the Blackened Tilapia (page 106).*

3 large red onions
3 or 4 tablespoons extra-virgin olive oil
Coarse salt and cracked black pepper, to taste
3 tablespoons dark brown sugar
4 tablespoons balsamic vinegar, divided

Cut the onions in half vertically, removing the papery outer layers. With the cut
sides down, slice the onions as thinly as possible.

Place the oil in a medium skillet over medium heat and add the onions; season
with salt and pepper. Add the brown sugar and 1 tablespoon of the balsamic
vinegar, stirring every few minutes.

As the mixture begins to turn a light golden brown, the moisture will begin to
evaporate. Add the remaining vinegar 1 tablespoon at a time, as needed.

After 15 minutes, lower the heat to medium low and continue cooking for
about 35 minutes. The longer the onions cook, the more you will need to stir
them. The onions should be a deep, rich brown. Taste and adjust the seasoning if necessary.

Serves 8v

● ● ●

I'M CONFESSIN'

If you chill your onions
for about an hour
in the fridge (or 20
minutes in the freezer)
before slicing, you can
skip the crying jag.

s'marvelous smoky ONIONS AND MUSHROOMS

I'M CONFESSIN'

The divas love a one-pan wonder. If you prepare meat before this recipe, remove it from the skillet, then add a splash of wine to deglaze the pan, adding rich flavor that makes this veggie sauté truly s'marvelous. Just keep the meat warm while you do your thing.

How do you handle a hungry man? Steaks, chicken, and gourmet burgers are dressed to kill with this sensational topper. Lulu says to pile it on when you've run up the charge card—Mr. Meat-and-Potato Head won't pout long.

1 large onion, cut in half and thinly sliced
3 to 4 cups sliced mushrooms of your choice
2 tablespoons olive oil
Coarse salt and cracked black pepper, to taste
¾ teaspoon liquid smoke
2 tablespoons prepared barbecue sauce
Splash of dry white or red wine

In a skillet, sauté the onion and mushrooms in olive oil over medium-high heat. Season with salt and pepper.

Add the liquid smoke, barbecue sauce, and wine, stirring to deglaze the delicious browned bits from the bottom of the skillet.

Cook until onions and mushrooms are tender and sauce begins to thicken, about 10 minutes.

Serves 8

passionate pantry RED SAUCE

The language of desire: a bubbling pot of tomatoes, crushed together with basil, garlic, and a generous pour of wine. A deceptively simple concoction, it speaks of commitment but is as capricious as a glance through the pantry: the opening of a can, a flick of dried herbs. You're only human, so grab some good bread and surrender to passion. Serve seductively with pasta and a flourish of extra-virgin olive oil.

6 tablespoons extra-virgin olive oil, divided
1 medium onion, finely diced
Coarse salt and cracked black pepper, to taste
10 garlic cloves, minced
4 tablespoons dried basil
2 (28-ounce) cans crushed tomatoes
½ cup dry white wine
2 bay leaves

In a pan large enough to hold all of the ingredients, heat 2 tablespoons of oil. Sauté the onion until translucent, seasoning with salt and pepper. Add the garlic and basil and cook for about 1 minute over medium to medium-high heat.

Pour in the tomatoes and wine and add the bay leaves. Season again with salt and pepper. Bring to a simmer; cover and cook for 1 hour, stirring occasionally. Taste and adjust the seasoning if necessary; drizzle in the remaining oil. Remove the bay leaves.

Serves a crowd

• • •

I'M CONFESSIN'

Good ricotta cheese (preferably whole-milk) seasoned with salt, pepper, and a drizzle of your best olive oil adds the diva dimension to ordinary noodles and sauce— and it couldn't be easier.

Waist not? *Want not.* Unless you're blessed with the metabolism and athletic skills of a cheetah, it's probably best to skip the sweet ending. Of course, there are exceptions: entertaining, special occasions, or the PMS-charged search and seizure of all things chocolate.

For dinner parties and other such calorie-rich occasions, indulge taste buds with a memorable and delicious finale. Here are some easy, stylish, and mostly homemade ideas that require minimum time in the kitchen and maximum time with friends and family.

SIZE DOES

MATTER

easy

● A simple chocolate truffle is one of the most extravagant indulgences in the world, a sensual ending that comforts and energizes all in one bite. Serve rich, dark chocolate truffles with sweet port, or with coffee and a fine cognac so that the chocolate doesn't compete with the aroma of the wine. Most gourmet groceries carry a good grade of dark chocolate candies—the best is at least 60 percent cacao solids.

● Rich Eiswein, or "ice wine," is always a pleaser, made from grapes left on the vine to freeze, then pressed before they thaw. Good ice wine is expensive, so save this option for very special occasions. Heavenly with perfectly ripe strawberries.

● Say cheese. A simple arrangement on a marble or granite slab is perfect. Arrange it an hour or so before serving, and let it rest in a cool place. Five nice contrasts are Cheddar, Parmigiano-Reggiano, Muenster, Stilton, and Bûcheron. Serve with fresh fruit and Sauternes, ice wine, or late-harvest Riesling for a blissful ending.

● Real whipped cream makes any dessert special, particularly fresh berries—strawberries, blueberries, peaches, or whatever is in peak season. You can soak the fruit in sugar syrup, wine, or liqueur to soften and sweeten it. For the whipped cream, use confectioners' sugar to avoid the grittiness of granulated sugar. Serve with a crunchy cookie or macaroon.

● Bake bananas. Peel and vertically slice six very ripe bananas. Arrange in a buttered baking dish and sprinkle generously with brown sugar (about 6 tablespoons), and sprinkle with cinnamon. Dot with butter. Bake at 400° for 15 minutes or until bubbling and brown. Serve with vanilla ice cream and a splash of rum.

● Bake apples. Choose tart green apples and core them. Put 2 tablespoons of butter and 1 tablespoon of brown sugar in each apple, then sprinkle with cinnamon. Bake at 375° for 15 minutes or until apples are tender.

● Make chocolate fondue. Over a pan of boiling water, melt half a pound of semisweet chocolate or semisweet chocolate chips in an ovenproof mixing bowl, stirring occasionally. Meanwhile, melt ¼ cup salted butter in the microwave. In the bowl with the melted chocolate, whisk together the butter and

½ cup heavy whipping cream. (No need to keep this fondue hot, as the butter and cream keep it from solidifying.) Serve with chunks of fresh pineapple, bananas, strawberries, cubed pound cake, and pretzel rods. Or drizzle over your bakery's cheesecake.

easier

● Make your own ice-cream sandwiches. Bake slice-and-bake cookies, then freeze for 5 minutes. Put softened ice cream on one cookie, and top with a second cookie. Roll in sprinkles, then refreeze until ready to serve.

● Brownies (use a boxed mix) with a scoop of good vanilla ice cream and a dollop of real whipped cream.

● A graham-cracker crust from the grocery store filled with your favorite flavor of softened ice cream (coffee is delicious). Top with crumbles of chocolate-toffee candy bar, refreeze, and slice.

easiest

● Buy a jar of hot fudge to top a scoop of premium vanilla ice cream. All the better with a flourish of real whipped cream.

● Brew a pot of good roast coffee and serve with a buttery tart from your favorite baker.

index

index

index